CREATIVE EDUCATION
AT AN ENGLISH SCHOOL

CREATIVE EDUCATION AT AN ENGLISH SCHOOL

BY

J. HOWARD WHITEHOUSE

CAMBRIDGE
AT THE UNIVERSITY PRESS
MCMXXVIII

CAMBRIDGE
UNIVERSITY PRESS

University Printing House, Cambridge CB2 8BS, United Kingdom

Cambridge University Press is part of the University of Cambridge.

It furthers the University's mission by disseminating knowledge in the pursuit of
education, learning and research at the highest international levels of excellence.

www.cambridge.org
Information on this title: www.cambridge.org/9781107455931

© Cambridge University Press 1928

First published 1928
First paperback edition 2014

A catalogue record for this publication is available from the British Library

ISBN 978-1-107-45593-1 Paperback

To

my friend
The Very Reverend William Ralph Inge
Dean of St Paul's

this tribute of admiration
and gratitude

CONTENTS

ILLUSTRATIONS

ILLUSTRATIONS

ILLUSTRATIONS

WOODCUTS

Chapter 1

TO THE GENERAL READER

FOR many years it has been my privilege to take part in the conference of educational associations held annually in London. I have frequently been struck at that conference by grave and serious statements made by leaders in the educational work. I heard the former headmaster of one of the greatest public schools declare that public schools had failed to interest their boys in acquiring knowledge. I heard another eminent man record his conviction that the failure of the schools to awaken interest was repeated at the universities, and he described the joy with which undergraduates with whom he had been associated burned their books after passing an examination: they would rather have the joy of seeing them burn than of selling them. These are two examples of innumerable ones which could be quoted.

These things show that there is something wrong in some of our methods of education to-day, so far as those methods fail to arouse any response from the pupils. I am, however, far from thinking that there is a general failure on the part of English schools. I believe that experiment is more widely prevalent than ever before and throughout many schools of the country much new work is being done on fresh lines with results wholly beneficial to pupils and to masters, and through them to the country.

I think nothing but good is done by the sharing of experience. That is one thing which makes educational conferences of enduring value. The machinery in this country for the recording of experiment and experience is not great. In the United States there is far greater popular interest in the problems, experiments and development of education. It is easier there to discover what is being done. In this country we greatly need a clearing house of ideas. Perhaps in the future the Board of Education may increasingly fulfil this office. The work of the Special Enquiries branch of the Board, under Sir Michael Sadler, filled many persons engaged in education with hope. I am sure that many regret that the work of that branch was not greatly extended and particularly that the system of issuing reports, not only on educational work in foreign countries, but on developments in this country, was not more extensively practised.

In the present book I have tried to set forth some of the things we have attempted at Bembridge. I hope one possible school of critics will accept a statement I should like at once to make. In issuing this little book, we make no claims of any kind: we make no reflections or criticisms upon others, and we have no wish to do so. Having received help from others, we desire to record some of the things we have done and the methods we have tried, in case they are of help or encouragement to anyone else. Many schools may already have done some of the same things. But it may not be without interest or value to attempt to set forth the creative activities of a school where, without, we hope, any weakening of the literary and academic side of education, arts and crafts, to quote an old phrase of my own, are regarded as instruments of spiritual and intellectual education.

I should like to attempt to define what I mean by creative education. I mean by this phrase that form of education which, whether it consists of manual activities or of other activities, is attempting to enable a child to develop his own personality, to find out through activities the things he can do, and that interest him and are going to give him a fuller and richer life.

Sir Michael Sadler made an eloquent appeal at the beginning of the present year for better methods of enabling students of education to find out what was being done in the newer schools of the country as well as in the whole field of educational ex-

2

periment. He mentioned Bembridge among other schools, and this book is a response to that and other suggestions.

But it requires some courage for the staff of a school to set forth some of the things they are trying to do, and the experiment would be impossible if their motive was misunderstood.

I have been always particularly anxious in connection with Bembridge that every boy in the school should have around him such an atmosphere, with the necessary facilities, as will enable him to give full and free play to his own personal interests and hobbies. Only in this way can a boy develop the possibilities within him; only in this way can he acquire a feeling for those real values in life, which, later, will distinguish him, in all vital ways, from the ignorant and the illiterate, no matter how athletic these may be. I believe profoundly that manual activities—using these words in their widest sense to embrace art and craftsmanship—should not be regarded as trivial "extras" or as pastimes for young children, but should be given a place of honour in every school, as in every other community, and should be recognised as definite instruments of noble education.

Such an ideal has always been in front of us here, and so far as we have been enabled in any degree to realise it, this has been without loss to the ordinary academic work common to all public schools. We believe, indeed, that the latter has greatly benefited, owing to the larger vision, the keener intellectual spirit, introduced into the school by a wider curriculum giving to arts and crafts their proper place.

Chapter 2

THE SCHOOL MUSEUM AND ART GALLERY

IN describing the various experiments through which we have tried to give to every boy the opportunity of developing his own special gifts, and thus of expressing more fully his own personality, I ought perhaps first to deal with the school museum and art gallery. This has been organised on new and perhaps novel lines. We do not regard the museum as a place wherein to store a number of objects whose dusty antiquity soon ceases to inspire any interest. The main principles we have observed in connection with the museum are these. We have held different exhibitions each term; we have always kept one term each year for an exhibition of boys' work; we have associated the boys with the management of the museum and, between the special exhibitions we hold, we have shown our permanent collection of pictures.

The museum was founded in 1919. Since that time we have held each term a special exhibition illustrative of a definite subject. Each summer term the exhibition consists wholly of the work of the boys of the school, executed during the previous year, and includes work done in all branches of the curriculum. In the other terms no limit is placed upon the subjects which may be chosen as the object of the exhibition. The range of subjects dealt with will be seen from the following list of the exhibitions held since 1919:

1920
Autumn Term. Bembridge School Exhibition.

1921
Spring Term. Drawings by Viennese Children.
Summer Term. History of the Isle of Wight and School Exhibition.

Autumn Term. National Arts and Crafts.

1922

Spring Term. Model Engineering Exhibitions.
Summer Term. School Exhibition.
Autumn Term. Water Colour Drawings by Sydney Carter.

1923

Spring Term. Decorative Art and Furniture.
Summer Term. School Exhibition.
Autumn Term. National Photographic Exhibition.

1924

Spring Term. Posters.
Summer Term. School Exhibition.
Autumn Term. Sheffield Museum Loan Collection.

1925

Spring Term. Scientific Society's Exhibition.
Summer Term. School Exhibition.
Autumn Term. Drawings by Ruskin.

1926

Spring Term. Minerals and Fossils.
Summer Term. School Exhibition.
Autumn Term. Drawings by T. M. Rooke.

1927

Spring Term. Scientific Society's Exhibition.
Summer Term. School Exhibition.
Autumn Term. National Arts and Crafts.

1928

Spring Term. Drawings by Albert Goodwin and others.
Summer Term. School Exhibition.
Autumn Term. American Architecture.

The holding of these exhibitions has led to many desirable results. The most important are, I think, these. They have meant that a new interest is always coming into the life of the school, and thus freshness of outlook is encouraged. Boys who are interested in different arts or crafts have the opportunity of seeing examples of the best work which is being done in the directions in which they are interested. Thus they receive encouragement and suggestion. This is especially true in connection with the exhibitions of national arts and crafts which have been held, for here we were able to gather together some of the finest examples of art and craftsmanship which were being done in the country. We were always conscious of the increased artistic interest which followed such exhibitions.

Occasionally the responsibility for organising an exhibition has been taken by one of the school societies. The Scientific Society has organised several. In these, many of the exhibits were made or prepared by the members of the society, and in this way a boy's scientific interests have been greatly fostered and stimulated.

An exhibition like the one illustrating the history of the Isle of Wight is particularly valuable because it enables so much practical work to be done by the boys in history, geography, literature, geology, and other subjects. Literary, historical and geographical maps of the island were prepared, fossils and other specimens were collected, old maps were copied, drawings of cliffs, showing strata, were made, and in these and many other ways the preparation of the exhibition was an important cultural influence.

In connection with pictures, the object of many of the exhibitions has been to bring before boys examples of good pictures worthy of their admiration, and to encourage their understanding of them. All the exhibitions have been accompanied by explanatory lectures, and small groups of boys have been taken round the exhibition as frequently as they wished for more detailed study.

Whatever may be said as to the value of these special exhibitions there can be no doubt that the annual exhibition of

6

the work of the boys of the school has been a source of great help and encouragement to all the school. A boy has been encouraged to submit the best work he could do, not from any undue pride of authorship, but as the expression of his own special interests and as a contribution to the common work of the school. It has been good to see the absence of rivalry or jealousy, and the unaffected delight shown by all the school in pieces of specially good work perhaps done by boys having exceptional ability.

These exhibitions of school work have also enabled the authorities of the school to form a judgment as to the influence various activities were having not only upon the individual, but upon the school and that indefinable thing, the school spirit. In not a few cases they have enabled a boy's friends to advise him rightly as to his future career.

I have stated that it is a feature of the museum to associate the boys with its management. This has meant an increase in the usefulness of the museum. It has increased a sense of responsibility on the part of the boys concerned. It has provided yet another interest for them. Two boys act as curators of the museum. Other boys are associated with various exhibitions and help in the arranging and hanging of exhibits.

Some of the happiest little social gatherings I remember took place one winter term when, on Sunday afternoons, we had small groups of boys to tea in the museum, and after tea inspected in detail a little collection of pictures and discussed questions of art which arose.

Chapter 3

THE PLACE OF DRAWING

AT Bembridge, in common I hope with some other schools, drawing is taught to every boy in the school at every stage of his school life. It is not expected that every boy will become an artist, or that he will desire to adopt art as a profession in later life. It is hoped that as a result of his practical work in drawing every boy will ultimately have a new means of communication and of self-expression.

To instance the greatest modern example of the value of drawing in the life of the individual, much of the work of Ruskin would never have been written had it not been for the training in careful drawing which he had as a boy. He was thus taught accurate observation, and given an instrument by which he could record beauties and details in art and nature as he perceived them from day to day. His note books, full of rough sketches, were to him what commonplace books, full of verbal descriptions, would be to others. More than this, in the greatest of his books, he was able to increase their value, and, indeed, to make their writing possible, by the illustration of his theories by the work of his hands. The world owes more than it realises to the patient practice of drawing in the education of Ruskin from a very early age.

We have tried many ways of interesting boys in drawing and in relating it as far as possible to other subjects and interests. It has, for instance, often been done in connection with nature study, and the life of flowers and trees has been recorded. It has been related to literature. One happy scheme which was undertaken in this connection was the preparation of books illustrating great poems or tales. The *Ancient Mariner* and various fairy tales were produced in this way, different boys undertaking to do certain pages or sections. In this way a group

8

spirit was obtained. The books which resulted were bound and preserved.

Our work in drawing has included the copying of details of pictures by great artists. This again has taught accurate observation as well as the true appreciation of good and great work.

The question of developing originality in boys in connection with drawing is an important one, and also difficult. There are many boys who have no original power who yet gain greatly by the practice of drawing. It gives them a new means of amassing experience, thus supplementing reading and writing. It trains hand and mind. It has an enduring value. The fact, therefore, that a boy shows no power of originality should not be regarded as a reason for not teaching him drawing. It would be like limiting reading to boys of special gifts or insight. But there are many boys who can be helped to express their power of originality in drawing. To such every encouragement is given. A considerable part of the work in drawing gives full play to a boy's power to express himself.

Chapter 4

WOODCUTS

ANUMBER of woodcuts appear in this book. The art of woodcutting appeals to many boys when they have the opportunity of understanding something about it and of practising it. Two years ago I had the privilege of issuing a book containing fifty examples of their work. The woodcuts now shown have been executed since that book was published, and I may be allowed to reprint a few passages from the introduction which I wrote to the book, for they express what I felt then and now to be the truth.

What gives me special pleasure in connection with the contents of this little book is the fact that they do not represent the results of the compulsory practice of the subject. The work done is the reflection of the interests of the boys concerned, and they have found time for it outside the school time-table and the demands of the form room. Some of the boys whose work is shown have inherited their interest from homes where art is loved and practised. All of them have been able to avail themselves of the advice and criticism of the Head of the Arts and Crafts department of the school, and have been able to count upon every encouragement in their work.

The interest of the wood-engravers has been greatly stimulated at Bembridge owing to the fact of the existence of the private printing press installed at the school. Upon this press the boys print each term the school newspaper, and the greater part of the woodcuts in this book were executed for it and have appeared in its pages. The boy engravers provide a fresh design for the cover of each number, and some of these cover designs are given.

Perhaps I ought to anticipate one criticism by stating that we are aware of the distinction between woodcuts and wood-engravings, and in using the former word as the title of this chapter we are following the example of many masters who use the term to cover both processes.

If my friends will allow me I should like to emphasise a few points in connection with this craft which appear to me worth consideration in attempting to assess its educational value.

It is the earliest and simplest form of reproduction known, and the whole process can be carried out by the craftsman. He draws the design, engraves it upon the wood, and prints his own block. The fact that he is master of the situation, responsible for the whole of the processes, gives him a special interest, sometimes amounting to fascination, in the work.

The fact too that he controls the whole operation gives the young craftsman the opportunity for a fine lesson in forethought and concentration. He cannot rub out as in sketching. In working on wood he must think before he acts, for a momentary loss of control may wreck the whole of his work.

The technique of cutting and engraving requires a steadiness of hand, and nice control of the tool, which is in itself an un-equalled manual training. The process sets definite limitations to the design, limitations which are easily grasped by a mind not sufficiently mature to understand the advantages of arbitrary and self-imposed limitations.

All creative interests which come into the lives of boys are good and may prove of transcendent importance. It is not that we want a boy to cut woodblocks in order to get his living when a man as a wood-engraver, any more than we desire a boy who loves flowers and creates a beautiful garden to become a professional gardener. Such boys in following these and other creative activities are unconsciously forging keys unlocking for themselves the entrance to courts of beauty and of joy—the beauty of all true work, the joy of service and self-realisation expressed in all true work, and to these courts they come with standards of taste and judgment achieved through personal effort and experience, not docilely received from others.

I do not wish to use language of exaggeration when I speak of the influence upon a boy of the craft illustrated in this book, but I am recording a personal belief based upon careful observation when I state that the designing and cutting of these blocks have meant for the boys who made them not only greater facility of hand and eye but enlarged powers of appreciation of nature, architecture, and the poetry of the world around us.

Chapter 5

THE INFLUENCE OF A PRINTING PRESS

OF the manual activities for boys, I should place very high those associated with the printing press. Nine years ago we installed a hand press in the school, and since then this has been the centre of many important educational activities. Each term we have produced a large magazine, entirely set up and printed by the boys, and illustrated with woodcuts done by the boys. All the younger forms have one or more periods weekly in the printing room.

I should like briefly to state some of the advantages which I think arise from the possession by boys of a printing press.

It has given a new interest to many of them in their English work, and especially in creative English work, through being able to set up in print things written by themselves or their friends. Quite unconsciously it has improved their spelling and their literary style, owing to the precision necessary in the operation of printing. But I put first the encouragement of the creative spirit in their English work.

A second important result is that by printing in the historic method, following the example of the first printers in the arrangement of their pages, in observing perfect simplicity and in abstaining from mixing types, they have acquired from experience a certain standard, simple it may be, of taste and criticism which has an influence far beyond the limited subject of printing.

A third important result which I notice with great interest is that practising a great craft and realising at first hand something of what it means, the boys are enabled to look through a window—a little window it may be—but to look through a window upon the great world of industry and to understand in a way they could not do otherwise something about industry and those who follow it.

But mark what follows. I have always felt that one of the great problems of schools and of educationists and of all who have the care of the young, is to give them real interests which will fill up their spare time whilst they are young, and which will give them real interests and lead them to other and greater interests when they are grown up. And all creative activities which children are allowed to follow at school have this immediate advantage, that they solve the problem of leisure hours; they give them interests in their leisure time, the benefit of which in every way could scarcely be overstated: and as they grow older these interests extend.

If I take the example of the printing press, it is only one example I could take of many. I have seen this from my personal experience, that boys in their spare time, without any suggestion or compulsion of any kind, will come and make suggestions as to how they could use the press in their spare time, things they would like to write and then print upon it, things they would like to print for other boys, things they would like to print for the service of the school. So that there are some boys to whom it makes a special appeal, who are always to be found doing useful things in the printing room, printing things that they have written or that others have written, and finding a source of great education and joy in consequence.

Chapter 6

THE ACTIVITIES AROUND A WOODWORK SHOP

IN the woodwork room we have tried to adopt such methods as would enable some at least of the following ideals to be realised. We want to insure that every boy shall have a good working knowledge of the use of tools, that he shall be made as resourceful and independent as possible, and that he shall be given not only hobbies for his present spare hours, but real interests in his future life.

First let me describe the place the woodwork room occupies in the life of the school. The woodwork room is really a form room, where a great deal of creative work is done, and from whence many activities in connection with the school are organised.

Every boy spends certain periods in the woodwork room during the whole of his school life, beginning by going through all the stages of simple carpentry. As soon as a boy has the necessary skill he is associated with other boys in doing a definite piece of work, which gives him further training, associates him with a little group, and encourages public spirit by doing work for the good of the community. Members of the school have made simple furniture, have executed repairs, erected a simple building in brick, and a more ambitious one in wood.

These are all things which they do as members of the school, training themselves and at the same time doing things useful to the whole body.

But all these activities in the woodwork room lead on to something we regard as of equal or even greater importance. The woodwork room, with its tools and equipment, is open on half holidays and every evening, and any boy may use it to make anything he wishes, or do any reasonable piece of work.

The Head of the Arts and Crafts department is present to give expert guidance and advice. The result is that throughout the whole of every term the room is generally full of active, busy, happy boys, making things for their own use, or to send to their homes.

I was writing the foregoing words on a school half holiday, and I paused at this point to visit the room I am describing, to see what activities were going on. I walked first along the edge of our cliffs, and looked once more on a prospect so lovely as to defy description. There was the bluest of seas under a cloudless sky and a brilliant sun. There was just enough wind to cause the sea to respond with a slight caress. The cliffs were a brilliant burning mass of golden gorse. The line of rocks, covered at high tide, dark and stern in winter, cried out to be used as a playground. But to-day my attention as I passed was chiefly claimed by the sight of three tiny canoes sporting on the gentle waters. They had been made by boys in their workshop. The making of them had occupied many happy hours, and now their owners joyously rode them on the sea.

Then I went on to the woodwork room—we call it the Arts and Crafts room—and I found it full of busy boys. Three were making boats. One of the boats was an attractive tiny canoe, designed by the boy who was making it, and singularly graceful in its design. Another boy was making an aquarium; others a wireless cabinet, a set of bookshelves, a little house for strange creatures from the woods, a book trough, a gramophone.

I looked from the objects being made to the boy workers. Here was activity generating happiness, here were lives full of happy interests. I felt that some of the problems of the future were in course of solution.

Chapter 7

GARDENING AS A SCHOOL ACTIVITY

I HAVE ever been of opinion that the love of gardens and the making of them are the greatest of all hobbies. That is why I should like to feel that every boy at least has the opportunity of learning something of the elementary stages of the art, for otherwise its pleasures must remain unknown to most of them.

We have deliberately made gardening a school subject, and for all forms under the Upper IVth it has a place in the time-table. When we began the teaching of gardening we set apart a piece of ground and cultivated it in common. The method was, however, only moderately successful. Now we give to every boy except in the two top forms (some of whom, however, also join in the scheme) a plot of ground, for the cultivation of which he is responsible. He is taught in school hours how to make it into a garden, and he is required to keep the plot in order and to give it whatever care is necessary.

It is not an exaggeration to say that many boys—particularly the younger ones—acquire under this system a lasting love for gardens. There are a number of boys, of course, who look after their plots as a duty to be performed, sometimes with in-difference. But many show great efficiency and enthusiasm in developing their gardens and take additional plots.

We have tried to give boys who show an aptitude for the art some feeling for landscape gardening. One or two boys have been entrusted with pieces of ground which they can plan with a view to small landscape effects. A reproduction is given in this book from a drawing of one of these small landscape gardens. The boy responsible for this piece of work has also constructed the pool shown in the foreground. Since this drawing was made he has developed a rock garden around it.

One result of the place of honour given to gardening in our hobbies is an increased interest not only in the preservation of the beauty of our grounds but in schemes for making them more attractive.

There is a general interest in the development of our grounds, in the making of avenues of trees, and in the care and study of trees. There is, we think, some genuine pride felt in seeing virgin fields, and rough corners, turned into attractive places.

Chapter 8

THE WORK OF A SCIENTIFIC SOCIETY

WE have tried to interest boys in the problems of Science and especially of its recent applications in the service and enjoyment of man. We have therefore supplemented the class-room teaching with voluntary work done under the inspiration of a strong scientific society.

The society has done some original things and has tried new methods, but the ideal has been an old one—to inspire boys with the desire to pursue independent research and experiment.

During the autumn and winter terms a weekly meeting of the society is held, at which one of the boys gives a paper on a scientific subject. Here is a list of the subjects of the lectures given during one recent term. It is a typical list:

Earthquakes.
Water Power.
The Quest for Colour.
Michael Faraday.
Dr Nansen's Journey Farthest North.
Achievements of Electro-chemistry.
The Story of the Electric Lamp.
The Planets: Mars, Jupiter, and Saturn.
Gold: how it is Mined and Extracted.

With a view to further encouraging scientific interest, the best essays given before the society, or prepared without intention of being read to others, were printed and published a little time ago in a book entitled *Adventures in Science*. It may be of interest to set forth the contents of this book:

Introduction by the Warden.
Things we have done together, E. J. Baggaley.
The History of the Theory of Light, J. M. Foot.

The Manufacture of Iron and Steel, K. D. Roeder.
Coal and some of its Products, J. R. H. Moreland.
A Wireless Set, I. Shankland.
Air and its Relation to Breathing, J. R. H. Moreland.
Electric Furnaces, N. F. Dixon.
The Early History of Chemistry, D. K. Munro.
Some Properties of Liquids, C. S. Weatherhead.
The Methods of Determining the Velocity of Light,
    J. M. Foot.
Crystals and Crystallization, K. D. Roeder.
Petrol, N. Rocke.

Quite apart from any other interest or value the book may have, its preparation caused much interest in scientific work and reading. It had also a social value to our community. The boys responsible for the book met together frequently for purposes of consultation and comparison. Boys who could not write but who could draw were pressed into the service to illustrate the papers, and the book when completed stood for a great deal of happiness around a piece of educational work.

As a further illustration of what we have tried to do in the promotion of scientific interest I should like to quote the following passages from *Adventures in Science* taken from the chapter entitled "Things we have done Together," which was written by the Head of the science work of the school, Mr E. J. Baggaley:

"In addition to lectures and essays, the activities of the Society have included much practical work, including the making of models and the holding of exhibitions. The models have been illustrative of the work done in form and laboratory, and, while some were wholly connected with physical and chemical science, others were constructed as illustrations of the geographical work of the School. A brief description of some of the models follows:

"MODEL OF THE ISLE OF WIGHT

"This model was carefully made in order that it should be an exact reproduction—to scale—of the Isle of Wight. The altitudes were shown in the usual way, by cutting out sheets of cardboard, each sheet representing a 50-ft. contour line at successive levels above the sea. The sheets of cardboard were then fastened down, one upon the other, and the whole was covered with a thin layer of plaster of Paris. The plaster was painted green and then the roads, towns, etc., in appropriate colours.

"MODEL OF THE SCHOOL GROUNDS

"The school grounds were modelled from plaster of Paris, and though altitudes were not constructed by contours, a model, essentially accurate, was made. The school buildings were made to scale in wood and painted in their natural colours; and the hedges and trees from the usual materials used for such things.

"The plaster was painted in green to represent the grounds, and the playing fields, with cricket and football pitches, marked out to scale were shown. The southern boundary of the grounds is formed by cliffs and the latter were also included in the model, together with the bathing place on the sands below.

"MODEL OF A HILL-SIDE SPRING

"This model was built to illustrate the formation of a spring, and the geographical structure of a hill. It was contained in a wooden tray, and in order that the strata could be examined, the sides of the hill were enclosed by glass.

"The impermeable stratum was modelled from clay, and this covered the whole of the containing tray, which thus formed the bed of the stream resulting from the spring. The permeable stratum forming the upper part of the hill consisted, first, of sandy soil, and then a layer of fine gravel. This was covered with a little earth, and then turfs were placed over the entire hill and plain. Heavy rain was supplied from a watering can, and in a short space of time the permeable strata had become saturated and water appeared at the lowest junction of the permeable and impermeable strata. After a few heavy rains, the bed of the stream became well defined, and the narrow, shallow bed at first constructed, became widened and deepened,

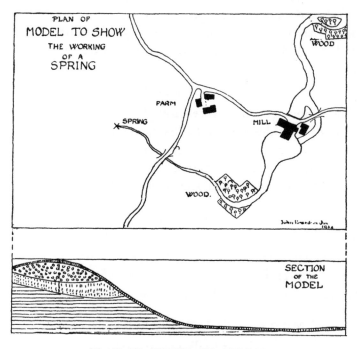

PLAN OF MODEL OF SPRING

with here and there a stone causing a waterfall. Down on the plain, a mill was built over the stream, some of the water passing from the mill-pond through the mill, the rest going over the weir. A farm, roads, and woods made from mossy twigs added to the attractiveness of the model.

"MODEL ILLUSTRATING THE HOT WATER SYSTEM OF A HOUSE

"This model was constructed at a time when convection of heat was being studied. The house contained four rooms, in one of which was a boiler, the others representing a bath-room, a drying-room, and a room heated by hot water pipes and radiator (the drawing-room). The boiler was adapted from the boiler of a model steam engine, and hot water was carried round the drying-room. The water passed on to the bath-room, and the drawing-room by means of a T tube, and then from the drawing-room back to the boiler.

"The bath-room, painted in white enamel, contained a bath fitted with hot and cold water, and it was this which attracted most of the attention of the boys, for it was a delightful room with its miniature taps, sponge, cork mat, soap and towel. The heating apparatus of the drawing-room consisted of glass tubing, painted black.

"The cold water supply was contained in a large tank in the roof, where the hot water tank and smaller cold water tank were situated. Accident was guarded against by the safety tube connected with the hot water tank.

"MODEL OF A GAS-WORKS

"In constructing this model an attempt was made to include as many of the operations of gas-making as possible, in order that it might have some resemblance to an actual gas-works. The retort consisted of hard glass tubing connected to a large flask containing cold water, which served as the condenser.

"The gas then passed up the coke tower—a tin containing coke—down through which water trickled; and then to the purifier, a small wooden box containing shelves covered with a layer of slaked lime. From the purifier, the gas was conducted to a simple gas-holder, the nature of which is well shown in the accompanying diagram.

"Considerable difficulty was experienced in obtaining a

23

sufficient supply of gas to ensure a constant flame at the jet, through which the gas passed after leaving the gas-holder.

"MODEL OF A COAL MINE

"This model represented a section of a coal mine in order that the shafts and the various strata with coal seams could be seen.

"Between the two shafts was the engine shed, the engine being employed to raise or lower the cage in one shaft, the coal bucket in the other, and to work a pump for the removal of water present in the pit. The engine caused a drum to revolve, and a rope, with its two ends attached to the cage and the bucket, was wound round the drum, the revolution of the drum thus raising the cage while lowering the bucket. The lower ends of the shafts were joined by a passage-way, this coinciding with a coal seam, and from this passage-way the galleries of coal separated by pit props could be seen, together with the lines along which coal trolleys are pushed.

"In a recent term, the Society undertook to prepare an exhibition to be held in the School Museum. During the earlier part of the term, many interesting exhibits were borrowed, models were made, and a number of experiments were prepared. The exhibits covered many aspects of science, particularly in its application to every-day life and its needs.

"The models made by the boys were an essential part of the exhibition, and the experiments dealt with the spectroscope, vacuum and spectrum analysis tubes and fluorescence, the composition of white light, silver, nickel and copper plating, anaglyphs, syphon and fountain showing the principle of the hydraulic ram, Roget's spiral, gas mantle photography, etching of metals and glass, surface tension, sounding tubes, vortex ring, invisible inks, absorption by platinum, and iodides."

Chapter 9

THE WORK OF AN ART SOCIETY

WE have tried to consolidate the art work of the school by the formation of an Art Society, in which all boys with special artistic interests take part.

During the autumn and spring terms regular meetings are held, when papers on art subjects are given by the boys. Here is a list of the papers given during one recent term:

Schools of Art through the Ages.

Manuscripts and the Scriptorium of the Middle Ages.

The Book of Kells.

What an Art Society might do.

Principles of Modelling.

The Pre-Raphaelites.

The members of the society are intimately associated with the exhibitions in the school museum and become a sort of unofficial committee. The main work of the society has, however, been the discussion of art problems and history. They have watched the contemporary press for important articles and illustrations dealing with art, and these are exhibited on a notice board kept by the society for the encouragement of general interest in art subjects.

In connection with the weekly meeting of the three head forms for the study of contemporary events, special attention has been given to questions of art and architecture, schemes for civic improvements, and the making of new bridges. Thus a boy's interest in art has been given as wide an horizon as possible.

In the case of some of the art exhibitions held in the school museum, to which detailed reference is made elsewhere, it has been the custom to invite little groups of boys to informal tea parties at the museum in order that exhibits may be examined in greater detail and the intelligent interest of the boys secured.

It has happened naturally that the chief members of the art society have been of great help at these meetings.

Side by side with the art society, a sketching club has carried on active work. It has been the custom to hold weekly exhibitions on Sunday mornings of the work done during the week, the art master acting as assessor.

All the work done by the society should be considered in relation to the form-room work as described in another part of this book.

Chapter 10

LITERARY ADVENTURES

FEW subjects offer greater opportunity for original work than literature. Many schools have shown what can be done by the encouragement of individual initiative. Plays, poetry and essays are the ordinary literary work of a large number of schools, and in some schools many activities of a literary kind are centred around the school magazine.

We have been helped at Bembridge by the possession of a printing press, described elsewhere, on which not only the school magazine is printed, but other things. Addresses given at the school by distinguished visitors have been printed by the boys and have added to their literary interests. In some cases boys have printed on the press little books of poems or of essays of their own composition. The press has therefore been a centre of activities, wider than mere printing.

One of the most important literary experiments we have made was the production of a book relating to the historical and other features of the country in which our school is placed.

A number of boys founded a society for the study of local history. A series of meetings were held, various subjects were allotted to different members to study and write upon, and at later meetings the papers prepared were read and criticised.

The results of the work of the society were published under the title *Bembridge, an Historical and General Survey*. The book was published not as an example of antiquarian knowledge, or scholarly research, but as the record of a co-operative experiment, voluntarily undertaken, which not only gave pleasure to those who took part in it, but by stimulating interest in local history and traditions, encouraged those who took part in the work to care for the larger aspects of history and social relationships.

Perhaps the most valuable part of the experiment was to be found in the impetus which it gave to intellectual interests pursued under the conditions of true co-operation, conditions, too, which enabled each boy to work at something which reflected his own interests, and in doing so to enlarge them and, it may be, to acquire others.

The scope of the book will be best understood from the following list of the subjects of the chapters composing it:

Sketch of the history of the island.

The Roman occupation.

Bembridge, King Alfred and the first naval battle.

The physical history of the island.

Local legends.

Seashore life.

Bembridge fishermen.

The birds of Bembridge.

The herring gulls on Culver cliff.

Agriculture and plant life.

Yaverland church.

Literary associations.

Bembridge to-day.

There were also photographs and drawings reproduced in the book.

A book such as this enables a good many interests to be drawn together. Thus, for example, the boys interested in natural history were able to take over a section of the book and record the results of their special interests.

Another book written by the boys was entitled *Prose, Poetry and Pictures*. At the time when the contents of this book were written or drawn, the authors' ages varied from fourteen to seventeen. Their work, though sometimes abbreviated, was printed without other alteration, and as none of them knew that its publication was contemplated, it was sincere and un-affected. It was of value in showing that the literary and historical work of a school can be related to and united with interests in the great drama of events in the contemporary world.

We have found by experience that a good way of cultivating literary interests is to encourage boys to keep commonplace books and to enter in them extracts from books as they read them, poems that they are fond of, and in fact almost anything that represents their own interests. A large number of boys out of those given the opportunity have kept admirable commonplace books. A page from one of them is reproduced in this book.

One of the forms—a small one and containing many intimate friends—has recently co-operated in producing a little book entitled *A Form Room Fellowship*. It happened by chance that the boys of this form were nearly all boys possessing distinct literary or artistic interests. They all decided to make some contribution to a little book to mark their life as a form. The little adventure added to their interest in work, it made the form a very friendly and intimate place, and it set a certain standard of literary achievement for subsequent members of the form to live up to.

It is of course a commonplace to state that literature can be united with the study of other subjects. It is obviously essential that the study of history must go hand in hand with that of literature. I should like to offer a suggestion to help the study of both subjects. I refer to the use of charts made by the student himself. This is done to a little extent and such charts are also appearing sometimes in textbooks. We have used them with success.

A word of warning is perhaps necessary. They must not take the part of original reading and study. Their function is to aid the memory and imagination, not to be a substitute for these. A boy who has made a chart illustrating either any author he is studying, or any period of history, may get a grasp of the bearings of his subject possible in few other ways. For example, a chart made by a boy is reproduced in this volume illustrating the life and times of Shakespeare. The preparation of this chart accompanied a study of Shakespeare's plays and of the life of the dramatist. As will be seen, the chart raises all sorts of interesting historical and literary questions. With such a chart before him a boy quickly gets an understanding of the outlines of his subject and can fill in the details.

We have tried a method in connection with the school library which has led to good results in connection with reading. All boys are fond of reading. A smaller number are fond of reading literature. Some boys ideas of literature are confined to the works of Mr Edgar Wallace. Each boy in the school has a period allotted to him each week for reading in the school library a serious book of literature. The choice is his own, but it is approved. In this way many boys are taught the habit of reading and continue it in their leisure hours.

Chapter 11

THE PRACTICE OF POTTERY

AMONGST the arts and crafts we have given boys the opportunity of learning, we have found pottery of much educational influence. Any boy who wishes may use the pottery and receive instruction from the master controlling it. This art is practised outside ordinary school hours, usually in the late afternoon or evening, each boy coming according to a time-table. In this way his attendance at the pottery is so regulated, that it does not interfere with his play and other interests.

The accompanying illustrations show some of the pottery which has been produced, and the kiln in which it was fired. It is difficult to state exactly the result of the practice of pottery in the case of schoolboys, but it may be said without any sort of reservation, that certain good results have followed. It is an art which appeals to the active boy, as well as to the boy who is fond of quiet pursuits. The difficulties of one of the first processes in pottery, that known as "throwing," in which the boy works the clay on the wheel, make it adventurous and interesting.

The art is an extremely good training in patience and in the overcoming of difficulties. It has also great value as a means of cultural education. In the best of all ways a boy learns the meaning of beauty of form and colour, and under wise guidance is soon able to acquire standards of taste and criticism, and to be able to defend those standards. The boys learning pottery usually make their own designs for the decoration of their work, and it is therefore possible to treat the art of pottery in a synthetic manner, and to unite it with the teaching of drawing and design.

In letting boys practise pottery we are not seeking to train professional potters. We are allowing boys to add another hobby to their occupations and one which trains both hand and eye, and adds greatly to their artistic equipment.

Chapter 12

GUIDE POSTS

WHEN visiting the secondary schools of the United States I was impressed by the use which is made of the morning assembly. Some of the secondary schools in New York contain 5000 pupils. They are worked in two shifts, the first shift beginning work at 8 a.m., the second at midday. A feature of these big schools and of many of the smaller ones is the use of the general assembly for the purpose of individual training along certain lines. It is, of course, impossible in these big schools to have an assembly of the whole school. It is the custom to have an assembly of half the school at a time, or perhaps less than half. The assembly is managed by the pupils themselves. One of them presides. The proceedings are carried through with great precision. Minutes are accurately kept and carefully read. Short addresses are given. The whole organisation becomes an important training and develops individual initiative and responsibility.

At Bembridge we have started what we call Guide Posts. These are a series of short addresses given after prayers at morning assembly. Our object was to get almost every boy in the school to give in turn a short address of from one minute to three minutes in duration, and upon any subject the boy cared to choose. The system has proved successful, and for many mornings each term these short addresses have been given. It brings a fresh note of interest into the proceedings each morning. It is admirable for training boys to become accustomed to speaking before an audience without nervousness. It has directed the attention of the school to many aspects of outdoor life, for, as the name implies, we try in these talks to direct the attention of our audience to things they may see around them, with a view to encouraging observation, and reading. A boy generally chooses to speak on some hobby or subject in which he is specially interested. His little address only takes a minute or so, for we have not more time to spare for the purpose, and therefore the preparation of the address is not a serious item so far as time is concerned. Yet short as the address is, it has proved a most valuable training in speaking with great precision, brevity and clearness.

The following were all subjects of Guide Post talks in one term, and they are printed here to show the range of the voluntary selection made by the boys:

The Sea, Clouds, Noises in Nature, Wind, Effect of Wind on Vegetation, Windmills, The Oak Tree, Yaverland Manor, Atmosphere, Sunrises and Sunsets, Wild Flowers, Buoys, Culver Cliff, Whitecliff Bay, Heavy Scented Flowers, Thunderstorms, Tormentil, The Privet Hawk Moth, Mushrooms, Brading Harbour, The Queen Bee, Winged Seeds, The Song Thrush, Land and Sea Breezes, The Ash Tree, The Gold Crested Wren, Gulls, Orchids, The Flight of the Starling, The Cinnabar Moth.

The following are actual examples of the talks which have been given:

WILD FLOWERS

A Guide Post by C. H. D. ACLAND

Acting as a Guide Post this morning, I am going to talk about wild flowers. I think some people are inclined to think too little of them. Imagine, if you can, going for a walk without them—no buttercups and daisies, and no bluebells in the woods. Remember too that all trees and grasses are really wild flowers. I think you will soon find that you are not sufficiently imaginative.

Here, at Bembridge, we have a particularly large assortment of flowers. Various plants prefer various soils and situations. Some will only thrive by the sea, such as Yellow-wort and Century, the yellow and purple star-shaped flowers out on the cliffs. Others are Samphire, Rest-harrow, Horned Poppy, and Thrift or Sea Pink. Others like Rock-rose, Bee Orchis and Valerian prefer chalk.

The Scarlet Pimpernel and the little bright yellow Tormentil live best in clay. There are others which like a sandy soil.

There are some flowers which live in woods because they like shade. Among these are the wild Iris, Bluebells, and Wood Spurge. There are yet others which prefer dry or wet, and, if you think for a minute, you will see that we have round us here, chalk, sand, clay, the sea-shore, woods and also dry and wet soils. All the flowers I have mentioned may be found quite near the school.

THE WOODPECKER

by J. R. BARKER

This morning I am going to say a few things about woodpeckers, more especially the Green Woodpecker. We are, I think, all familiar at least with its appearance and its cry, which is a harsh sort of cackle rather like the neigh of a horse. There are three kinds of woodpeckers found in England: the Green Woodpecker, the Great Spotted Woodpecker and the Lesser Spotted Woodpecker. The Green Woodpecker is bright green all over except for a crimson patch on its head. The Great Spotted Woodpecker has quite different colouring. It has a black-and-white back and wings, with a brilliant crimson patch on its breast which stands out against its otherwise rather dull plumage. The Lesser Spotted Woodpecker is smaller and has a somewhat similar colouring. It is much less common than the first two species and consequently not so generally interesting.

The habits of the Great Spotted Woodpecker are much the same as those of the Green Woodpecker. The Green Woodpecker lives in a hole in a tree and it is not particular what kind of tree so long as it is hollow or rotten in the centre. As this is very often the case when the outside wood is still quite sound, the woodpecker has some hard boring to do to get to the rotten centre, and if it is not reached at a certain depth, the site is forsaken and another one chosen. The hole is usually bored several inches horizontally and then from eight to twelve inches down into the rotten centre.

The eggs are usually five or six in number, very rarely seven or eight. These are laid on the chippings at the bottom of the tunnel. They are usually pure white in colour, sometimes with a creamy tinge, and the shells are transparent until they are blown. The young birds have no down, and consequently they bear a strong resemblance to tiny hedgehogs when they begin to grow some feathers.

One of the chief features of the bird is its strong and very solid beak which sometimes resembles a pick-axe in shape. It is used chiefly for boring holes in trees and also for picking insects from underneath the bark. These insects form its chief food. They are caught by means of a long pointed tongue which finds its way into the smallest crannies in the bark, and is covered with a glutenous substance at the tip to which the fat grubs and larvae stick, and are quickly consumed by the bird.

The young ones are at first fed by their parents on half-digested food until they emerge from their nest and begin to find insects for themselves in the surrounding trees. It is obvious that the nest will get reasonably hot with five or six little ones in it, and no form of ventilation other than the doors. This is one of the main reasons for the quick development of the young workers in getting food for themselves as they leave their home at the earliest possible opportunity to fend for themselves in a new and cold, but infinitely larger and less stuffy, world.

Chapter 13

WRITING IN SCRIPT

ARISING out of art activities, the practice of script writing should be mentioned. All boys in their earlier forms are taught script, by which I mean that ceremonial form of writing sometimes referred to as lettering, sometimes as writing, sometimes as print-script. But the description is taken from the old scriptorium where the manuscripts were written in those characters which in many cases remain as a joy to all who love beauty.

And this is the justification for the teaching of script—that it makes writing a very beautiful art and thus becomes not only a means to an end, but to some degree an end in itself.

I am not able to say with definiteness what is the extent of the influence of script writing on ordinary writing. It is a commonplace amongst all schoolmasters, and particularly amongst all parents, that most boys write badly. I believe myself that the boys who write the best script usually have a good style of writing which they ordinarily use.

But it is also true to say that many boys, particularly quite young boys, can write most attractive script whilst their ordinary writing is poor and crude.

The experiment I should like to see is the teaching of boys always to use a simple beautiful script for all their writing, instead of keeping script for special work. The practical objection to this course is that script writing takes, or is believed to take, far longer than ordinary writing, and the inexorable pressure of time is therefore apt to win.

I think it is reasonable to believe, and in my own case this belief is based upon several cases in my own experience, that where a boy is encouraged always to use script he develops quite naturally a beautiful handwriting in which the characters of script are kept and which he is able to write as quickly as he would an ordinary hand.

I am greatly interested in the beautiful work which a few boys are able to do in script. Some examples are given in these pages. In the case of at least one boy the love of this art is accompanied by a love of literature and the making of written anthologies. Thus literature and art go together.

Chapter 14

PLAYS AND THEIR PRODUCTION

I THINK it would be common ground amongst most persons engaged in education that the acting of plays was a great source of happiness to young people, and was also of considerable educational value. If I may instance the case of Shakespearean drama, although it is sometimes urged that the fact of the plays being so frequently made compulsory subjects for study and above all for examination has meant a positive dislike for Shakespeare, there is much more to be said about this study in schools. Where Shakespeare's plays are acted, the boys who take part in them, although they may be to a large degree insensible to their poetry, never regret in later years the learning of many portions of the plays. The memory of youth bears its burdens lightly, but it is a long memory, and there are not a few men and women to-day whose most precious literary possession is the power to repeat much of Shakespeare's poetry learned in careless years of long ago.

The acting of plays is therefore in many cases of more advantage than their study as textbooks for examination purposes.

We have at Bembridge a gymnasium which also serves the purpose of a theatre, and it has been our custom for many years to present a play each term, making a total of three new plays annually. In this respect we can be little different to many other schools. I only desire to mention two things we have attempted to do in connection with plays, which perhaps are worth recording. We have produced not only Shakespeare, but modern plays of distinction—by Masefield, Dunsany, Galsworthy, and others. The production of plays has thus been associated with the work we have tried to do in English literature. My belief is that the influence and value of the acting

39

of plays are greatly increased if there is a literary scheme in the background.

What is perhaps more important, we have tried to interest boys in the making of plays. In the following pages there is reprinted a little play performed by a few boys in French. This actual play is not written by a boy; it is the work of Mr Edward Daws, but the object and method of his writing and production are of educational value, and for this reason I call attention to it. The boys had read and discussed the exquisite little story by Anatole France. The master, who also took them in French, then adapted this little play from the story, taking with him the interest and co-operation of the boys in doing so. They then learned and acted it. I put aside the pleasure and group spirit created by this arrangement, but would point out the great help such a little experiment meant to the cultivation of a feeling and love for literature, and for a greater proficiency in a foreign language.

Members of the staff of the school or the boys have invariably designed all the dresses necessary for our plays and have made them. The boys have always been responsible for staging and scenery. Thus a whole group of healthy activities naturally form themselves around the production of a play.

Le Jongleur de Notre Dame

A FRENCH PLAY in four scenes adapted from the story by ANATOLE FRANCE

CHARACTERS

The juggler	1st monk
1st boy	2nd monk
2nd boy	3rd monk
3rd boy	4th monk
4th boy	5th monk
Beggar	The prior

1st scene: *In the* MARKET PLACE *of* AVIGNON
2nd scene: *Outside the* MONASTERY GATES
3rd scene: *In the* MONASTERY
4th scene: *In the* MONASTERY

SCENE I

A MARKET PLACE *in* AVIGNON, *about the year* 1300

A BOY *enters. He sings*

Au clair de la lune	Au clair de la lune
Mon ami, Pierrot,	Pierrot répondit:
Prête-moi ta plume	Je n'ai pas de plume,
Pour écrire un mot.	Je suis dans mon lit.
Ma chandelle est morte,	Va chez la voisine,
Je n'ai plus de feu,	Je crois qu'elle y est,
Ouvre-moi ta porte	Car dans sa cuisine,
Pour l'amour de Dieu.	On bat le briquet.

Enter ANOTHER BOY

2nd boy. Holà, Jean.
1st boy. Holà.

They play together. A THIRD BOY *enters*

3rd boy. Holà, Jean.
1st boy. Holà.
3rd boy. Savez-vous que le jongleur est en ville?
1st boy. Mais oui.
2nd boy. Comme je voudrais bien le voir. C'est peu probable. Il ne fait ses tours de passe-passe qu'au marché à midi lorsque nous sommes à l'école.
3rd boy. Quel dommage! Mais peut-être le rencontrons-nous, et il jouera exprès pour nous faire plaisir.
1st boy. Cela se peut bien. Nous n'avons pas d'argent à lui donner.

A CROWD *of* BOYS *enter*

Boys. Holà, Étienne et Jean.
1st boy. Holà.
2nd boy. Jouons au colin-maillard.
4th boy. Eh bien. Vous allez nous chasser.

They begin to play. At last JOHN *thinks he has caught one of them*

2nd boy. Ah. Je vous ai pris.

3rd boy. Non. Vous ne l'avez pas fait.

2nd boy. Vous êtes menteur.

3rd boy. C'est vous. Vous êtes tricheur aussi.

The TWO BOYS *fight, amid encouraging cries from the others.*
During the fight the JUGGLER *enters*

Juggler. Écoutez, mes enfants; taisez-vous.

1st boy. Ma foi, voici le jongleur. Monsieur, s'il vous plaît, voulez-vous nous faire un de vos tours?

Juggler. Mais oui, si vous vous entendez. Eh bien, mes enfants, mettez-vous en cercle. Il faut vous tenir tout à fait tranquil, pendant que je fais mon premier tour de passe-passe.

The JUGGLER *performs one of his tricks*

2nd boy. C'est merveilleux. Comment faîtes-vous cela?

Juggler. Maintenant je vais vous montrer comment je jongle avec les balles. En voici deux. Et, après, je veux que vous me chantiez quelque chose.

3rd boy. Oui, monsieur.

They sing together

> Il était un' bergère,
> Et ron ron ron, petit patapon,
> Il était un' bergère
> Qui gardait ses moutons.
>
> Elle fit un fromage,
> Et ron ron ron, petit patapon,
> Elle fit un fromage
> Du lait de ses moutons.
>
> Le chat qui la regarde,
> Et ron ron ron, petit patapon,
> Le chat qui la regarde,
> D'un petit air fripon,
>
> Si tu y mets la patte,
> Et ron ron ron, petit patapon,
> Si tu y mets la patte,
> Tu auras du bâton, ron, ron.
>
> Il n'y mit pas la patte,
> Et ron ron ron, petit patapon,
> Il n'y mit pas la patte,
> Il y mit le menton.

> La bergère en colère,
> Et ron ron ron, petit patapon,
> La bergère en colère,
> Battit son p'tit chaton, ron, ron.

Juggler. Merci, mes enfants. Encore, encore.

Song

> Enfin nous te tenons,
> Petit, petit oiseau,
> Enfin nous te tenons
> Et nous te garderons.
>
> Non, nous te donnerons,
> Petit, petit oiseau,
> Non, nous te donnerons,
> Biscuits, sucre, bonbons.
>
> Nous te gardons encore,
> Petit, petit oiseau,
> Nous te gardons encore,
> En cage en fils d'or.
>
> Tu dis la vérité,
> Petit, petit oiseau,
> Tu dis la vérité,
> Reprends la liberté.

3rd boy. Norman, vous chantez maintenant.
4th boy sings.

Song

> Écoutez bien l'histoire
> D'un Dieu dans un berceau.
> Gardez en la mémoire,
> Il n'y a rien de si beau.
>
> Dans une pauvre étable,
> Ce lieu n'est pas loin,
> Dans une paille sèche,
> Et sur un peu de foin.

Juggler. Merci, bien, mes enfants. Maintenant vous devez rentrer vite à la maison, car il est tard. Au revoir. Que le bon Dieu et la sainte Vierge vous bénissent. Ne vous vous fâchez plus.

2nd boy. Non, monsieur. Merci. Bon soir.

(They run off)

43

An OLD BEGGAR *enters*

Beggar. Les aumônes.

Juggler. Hélas, mon vieux. Je n'ai que très peu d'argent, mais je vous donnerai tout ce que j'ai.

Beggar. Que Dieu vous bénisse.

SCENE 2

Outside a MONASTERY

The JUGGLER *is seated at the roadside eating*

Enter a monk, BROTHER ANTOINE

Monk. Ce doit être le jongleur.

(He kneels at a SHRINE. *The* JUGGLER *joins him)*

> Notre Père, qui es aux cieux,
> Ton nom soit sanctifié,
> Ton règne vienne,
> Ta volonté soit faite
> Sur la terre comme au ciel.
> Donne-nous notre pain quotidien,
> Pardonne-nous nos péchés,
> Comme aussi nous pardonnons à ceux
> Que nous ont offensés,
> Et ne nous induis point dans la tentation,
> Mais délivre-nous du malin.
>
> Amen.

Juggler. Bonjour, mon père.

Monk. Bonjour, mon frère. Dites-moi, n'êtes vous pas le jongleur qui était à Avignon la semaine passée?

Juggler. Oui, mon père, je le suis.

Monk. J'ai entendu parler du bien que vous avez fait. Que Dieu vous récompense. Menez-vous une vie heureuse?

Juggler. Mais oui, mon père, la meilleure du monde. Mais quelquefois je n'obtiens pas assez de nourriture pendant l'hiver.

Monk. Non, mon frère, il y en a une qui est meilleure. C'est la mienne. Vous ne savez pas le bonheur de proclamer la gloire éternelle de notre seigneur Jésu-Christ et de la sainte Vierge et de travailler pour eux toute la journée.

44

Juggler. Non, mon père, mais un tel travail n'est pas pour les jongleurs comme moi-même. Je suis trop pauvre, et trop ignorant.

Monk. Non, mon frère, non, non. Il n'y a pas de service que la sainte Vierge n'accepte pas, et personne n'est trop pauvre à lui rendre hommage. Voulez-vous revenir avec moi?

Juggler. Oui, mon père, si ce que vous me dites est vrai, il n'y a d'autre chose au monde qui puisse me donner plus de joie. Je viendrai avec vous.

As they walk, they hear the sound of chanting

Song (off the stage)

Plaines et monts, chantez Noël, chantez Noël.

Juggler. Qu'est-ce qu'est cela?

Monk. Ce sont les moines au monastère. Ne connaissez-vous pas cette chanson? Je vous la chanterai.

Song

> Il est minuit.
> La lune éclair au loin,
> Les rives du Cédron.
> C'est l'heure sainte.
> Sur la terre déjà
> Court un divin frisson.
> Bethléem béni,
> Lève ton front dans Israel
> Pour naître Jésu, ton choisi.
> Plaines et monts, chantez Noël.

The PRIOR *enters*

Prior. Ah, mon cher Antoine, qui est cet homme aux habits verts?

Monk. C'est un jongleur célèbre, mon père. Mais c'est un honnête homme, et il veut demeurer chez nous pour être un de nos frères.

Juggler. Mon père, j'ai peur que je ne sois pas assez saint, mais j'aime notre dame et notre seigneur Jésu-Christ; si cela vous convient je viendrai rendre des services et travailler pour l'honneur du bon Dieu.

Prior. Vous viendrez, mon fils. Que le bon Dieu vous garde, et vous rendre heureux.

SCENE 3

The MONASTERY. *The* MONKS *are heard chanting in the chapel.*
A work room in the monastery

PRIOR *is heard off the stage*

Per te sciamus da patrem,
Noscamus atque filium,
Te utriusque spiritum
Credamus omni tempore.

The MONKS *enter*

1st monk. Voulez-vous nous chanter quelque chose avant que nous commencions à travailler.

2nd monk sings.

Song

Voici un mystère
Sur la terre qui va faire
Le bonheur de l'univers,
Dieu vient pour briser nos fers.

Gloria, gloria, in excelsis deo.

Que de chants d'allégresse
Dans les cieux que j'entends chanter
Sans cesse que gloire soit à Dieu,
La paix dans ces bas lieux.

The PRIOR *enters*

Prior. Comment avancez-vous dans votre travail, mon frère? Vous sculptez une image du saint enfant, n'est-ce pas?

3rd monk. Je crains que la pierre ne soit trop dur. J'ai peur de n'être pas assez habile à ciseler une roche si dure. Mais je ne suis pas inquiet, car je le ferai tout de même. Et d'ailleurs je suis heureux, très heureux.

Prior. Mes frères, avez-vous vu le frère qui est arrivé il y a quelques jours? Je veux que tous les assistants soient très gentils pour lui. C'est un jongleur célèbre, mais comme c'est un digne homme, et on parle bien de lui, je l'ai accepté comme membre de notre communauté.

4th monk. J'ai un grand respect pour vous, mon père, mais je crains que ce ne soit très dangereux. Nous n'avons aucun renseignement sur ce vagabond.

Prior. Vous avez oublié les mots de saint Paul.

N'oubliez point l'hospitalité car c'est par elle que quelques-uns ont logé des anges sans le savoir.

3rd monk. Mon père, il me semble que notre frère n'est pas heureux. Peut-être désire-t-il le calme de la campagne, le bleu des cieux, et la brise qui souffle de la mer.

2nd monk. Il désire peut-être les applaudissements des gens au marché et la rumeur de la ville.

1st monk. Il désire peut-être le commérage des brasseries, et les chansons des paysans pendant les moissons.

Prior. Je ne sais pas. Mais il a l'air d'un honnête homme. Quel magnifique teint, mon frère.

5th monk. Est-ce que vous l'aimez? J'en suis content. J'ai cherché ce teint, pour l'obtenir, pendant plusieurs années.

The JUGGLER *enters, very sad*

Prior. Pourquoi êtes-vous si triste, mon frère.

Juggler. Hélas, mes amis, je suis triste parce que je ne puis pas partager le bonheur de votre travail. Vous peignez, mon ami, ce tableau merveilleux de la sainte Vierge. Vous taillez, Guillaume, cette image du saint enfant. Moi, que puis-je faire? Je ne puis sculpter; je ne puis écrire; je ne puis peindre. C'est pourquoi je me sens triste, et j'ai peur de rester triste.

Prior. Restez tranquil, mon fils. Si vous aimez le bon Dieu, et si vous désirez à lui rendre hommage, ne doutez pas que vous trouviez le travail que vous désirez.

SCENE 4

In the MONASTERY. *Three weeks later*

1st monk. Ne le trouvez-vous pas étrange? Le frère, qui était jongleur, paraissait triste pendant les premiers jours chez nous, mais maintenant il est heureux, très heureux.

4th monk. Pourquoi était-il triste? Je ne comprends pas. Je me méfie de ce jongleur.

2nd monk. Il était malheureux parce qu'il ne pouvait rien faire pour la sainte Vierge.

3rd monk. Pensez-vous qu'il ait maintenant trouvé quelque chose à faire pour elle?

4th monk. Je ne sais pas. Peut-être oui. J'ai remarqué qu'il s'en va doucement à la chapelle après les matines.

2nd monk. Oui, c'est vrai. Je l'ai vu quand nous nous occupions à peindre et à sculpter.

3rd monk. Il revient toujours après quelques minutes, et il a l'air si heureux qu'il semble avoir eu une vision.

1st monk. Cela ne m'étonnerait pas. Il a le visage d'un ange, et l'esprit comme celui de notre seigneur Jésu-Christ. Quand je pense à lui je sais ce que le bon Jésu a voulu dire en disant ces mots: Laissez venir à moi les petits enfants et ne les en empêchez point, car le royaume de Dieu est pour ceux qui leur ressemblent. Je vous dis en vérité que quiconque ne recevra pas le royaume de Dieu comme un petit enfant n'y entrera point.

4th monk. Je voudrais le suivre pour voir ce qui arrive dans la chapelle. Je crois qu'il fait quelque chose de mal.

1st monk. Parlez bas. Le voici.

The JUGGLER *enters*

Juggler. Ah, mes amis, comme il fait beau aujourd'hui.

3rd monk. Il fait beau! Mais non, mon frère, il fait un temps terrible, et la pluie tombe à verse.

Juggler. Ah, il fait toujours beau à mon idée.

He goes out singing and goes into the chapel. After praying before the VIRGIN *he begins to juggle before her*

1st monk. Voulez-vous le suivre? Je me demande ce qui peut être son secret.

The MONKS *silently approach the door of the chapel, and peep through the door. The* PRIOR *also approaches*

4th monk. Mon Dieu, c'est blasphémer que de se conduire ainsi.

Prior. Mon frère, attendez un moment.

4th monk. Il faut mettre une fin à cette folie.

As they watch, while the PRIOR *restrains his brother monks, the statue of the* VIRGIN *comes to life, moves down the steps, wipes the sweat from the* JUGGLER'S *brow, blesses him, and returns to her seat*

Prior. Heureux les pauvres en esprit car le royaume de Dieu est à eux.

4th monk. Pardonnez-moi, mon père. Je suis pécheur. Je ne suis pas digne de lui porter les souliers.

Prior. Le bon Dieu vous pardonnera, mon fils.

The MONKS *enter and kneel in prayer around the* JUGGLER *and the statue of the* VIRGIN

Chapter 15

HOLIDAY OCCUPATIONS FOR BOYS

A FEW years ago we were confronted at Bembridge with the problem of the organisation of work of interest to boys during the holidays, particularly the long summer holidays.

We finally adopted the following scheme. A list of suggestions for holiday work was prepared and all boys were invited to carry out some of the suggestions. The house-masters corresponded with the members of their Houses during the holidays and encouraged them to find hobbies at which they could work.

The boys who took part in the scheme brought their work back at the beginning of term and it was exhibited in the school museum, book prizes being awarded for work of merit, and a list published in the school newspaper.

The scheme was very successful and some admirable voluntary work was done, though we found that more and better work was done in the summer holidays, and we finally confined the scheme to these.

Our list of suggestions became longer each year, passing from a few typewritten requests to a printed list containing seventy-five entries which were printed in full in *The Times* and other newspapers when they appeared. Their publication led to many inquiries as to the working of the scheme, and I have issued this pamphlet, by request, in response to many of those inquiries.

The list of suggestions has been extended to over one hundred, and explanatory notes have been added to the suggestions where it appeared that these might be helpful.

The great value of a scheme of this kind to a school lies in the fact that it encourages a boy to develop real interests in life, and to continue at home activities fostered at school. It may make the whole difference between a holiday of boredom and one of active happiness.

To all boys who read these few introductory words, I would only add this.

There is no happiness like that which comes to you from living a full life, doing real things. Games bring you great joy and properly fill some of the spaces of your time. They stand for health, and comradeship, and unselfishness, and giving you these things bring spontaneous joy into your lives.

But a life in which games were the only interest would be a barren life and would ultimately be left stranded before that court of the Kings of the world through the ages which all may enter who care for the expression of human activity in any of its many beautiful forms—books, pictures, craftsmanship, music.

These pages have been written in order to suggest ways by which you can develop your interest in a great number of creative activities, and in seeking to realise your own gifts in these and similar directions you will be raising your own body and soul daily into higher powers of duty and happiness.

SUGGESTIONS FOR HOLIDAY OCCUPATIONS

LITERARY

1. Write an account or criticism of any books which you read during the holidays.

2. Keep a diary of your holidays, illustrated if possible.

3. Keep a diary of important current events, illustrating it with cuttings from newspapers.

4. Write in a commonplace book extracts from poetry or prose which you would like to have permanently.

5. Obtain a copy of the local sheet of the 1-in. ordnance survey map. Visit interesting places shown on this map and describe them.

6. Essays on any subject that interests you.

7. Original stories or poems.

8. Write in script favourite extracts, with or without illuminations.

9. Make a classified catalogue of the books in your own library.

10. Describe any beautiful scenery near you and try to illustrate it.

11. Make a list of poets and writers connected with your county. Write out something written by each.

12. Describe any serious play which you see.

13. Make a list of famous men connected with your district. Add notes about each.

SCIENCE

14. Make a map of the district in which you spend your holidays.

15. Keep a daily weather chart.

16. Visit any quarries, pits, or mines near you. See the rocks below the soil. Examine the broken rubble, etc., for fossils. Write an account with sketches.

17. Keep a Nature diary day by day, recording your observations on any aspect of outdoor life.

18. Scientific models illustrating any process.

19. Chemistry. Make experiments of chemical processes, using simple home apparatus (e.g. Manufacture of Soap). Describe and illustrate these.

20. Write an account of any scientific discovery or of any pioneers in science.

21. Draw diagrams illustrating the working of a motor cycle or steam engine.

22. Construct a wireless set. Describe and illustrate it.

23. Visit a science museum and describe carefully one or more of the exhibits.

24. Pay weekly visits to the local library and read reports

of scientific developments contained in science periodicals. Summarise these.

25. Keep a diary of scientific phenomena which you observe—e.g. the scientific processes employed in road-mending, railway and tramway lines, the pulley, levers, etc.

26. Perform some of the simple experiments described in Sir Wm. Bragg's *The World of Sound* or Faraday's *Chemical History of a Candle*.

27. If a microscope is available, make studies of animal and vegetable pond-life, with drawings and notes of your observations.

28. Make a study of the work done by some of the famous scientists mentioned in science work at school.

29. Fit up a useful electric bell system in your house. Write an illustrated description of it.

30. Make a survey of your garden or other surroundings and build up a contour map from your observations.

31. Make up carefully the necessary solutions and do some silver or copper plating.

MUSIC

32. Music. Learn new pieces. Keep a list with brief account of any good music you hear during the holidays.

33. Make a collection of illustrations of musical instruments. Classify and describe them.

34. Make a list of the songs of Shakespeare, and find out the music that has been set to them. Music publishers would give you some of the necessary information.

35. Read a biography of any great composer, and make a chart connecting his life with the events of his time.

36. Read a book dealing with English folk songs, and learn typical songs of each century.

37. Learn one country dance tune or folk song from as many countries as possible. They can be obtained quite cheaply. Write a short description of each and attempt to account for

their national characteristics; e.g. the sadness of Russian songs, the military nature of many Alsatian songs.

38. If in London, go to hear the famous choirs at the Temple, Westminster, St Paul's, and other churches. Describe the music you hear there.

GARDENING

39. Make sketches or write an account showing how any gardening operations are performed—e.g. layering carnations, taking cuttings, trenching soil, budding and grafting, etc.

40. Draw a plan of a garden for a small house.

41. Plan a school plot six yards by three yards showing how you would stock it.

42. Draw a plan of a small public park. (You should make provision for its use by the public, games, etc., but you should also show how it can be made beautiful by landscape gardening.)

COLLECTIONS

43. Make a collection of photographs or illustrations of one or more of the following subjects: Architecture, scenes of natural beauty, churches, old buildings, birds, animals, flowers.

44. Make a collection of wild flowers, pressing them between blotting-paper, and mounting them on separate sheets.

45. Make a collection of details of trees—bark, leaves, flowers, fruit, wood. (Mount these on cardboard, carefully labelled.)

46. Make a collection of shells or fossils.

47. Make a collection of flowering grasses.

48. Make a collection of illustrations of as many kinds of boats and ships as possible—e.g. sailing, steam, motor, rowing, foreign, etc.

49. Make a collection of illustrations of old English furniture.

50. Make a collection of reproductions of great pictures. If possible, classify by country and school.

51. Make a collection of brass rubbings taken by yourself.

52. Make a collection of posters. (Many big firms and railway companies will supply examples at a very low price, or without charge.)

HISTORY, CHARTS, ETC.

53. Make a chart showing various facts in political, economic, and international history in parallel columns for any period you care to select.

54. Make a chart showing the dates of the most important inventions—e.g. printing, gunpowder, locomotives, etc.

55. Make maps of the routes of the great discoverers.

56. Make a number of tracings of maps of the world and show whence we get foodstuffs and other things.

57. Read a life of the most distinguished man of the period you are studying in form. Write an account of his life.

58. Read any diaries contemporary with the age you are studying. Write an essay showing what light these throw on the life of the period.

59. Discover the original sources for the history of your town or district. In any big town information can generally be obtained at the town hall or public library.

60. Compile an historical atlas illustrating the European history you are studying.

61. Make a list of all the great men of a given period who did not influence politics but who did influence art, literature, music, drama, science, medicine, or architecture. State briefly what they did.

HANDICRAFTS

62. Make any articles in wood or metal, and bring back to school either the articles or drawings or photographs of them.

63. Spinning, weaving, and dyeing. Bring examples.

64. Basketry. Bring examples.

65. Clay or Plasticine modelling. Bring examples.

66. Describe some of the arts and crafts carried out in your district.

67. Pottery. Collect illustrations of beautiful examples, giving date and other details.

68. Printing. Make a collection of pictures in as many different styles of reproduction as possible—half-tone, wood block, lithograph, line, etc.

69. Bookbinding. Re-bind an old book or the parts of a new one.

70. Make in wood a copy of some small detail from an old example—e.g. a carved panel, a door handle, a chair back.

71. Design your ideal day room for a boy. Show on the plan all the furniture you would like in it. (Provision for books, manual work, etc.)

PHOTOGRAPHY

72. Illustrate by photographs some manufacture carried on in your district—e.g. the making of a basket, chair, boat, house, etc.

73. Try methods of printing new to you—e.g. bromide, carbon, gas-light, platinotype. Bring examples.

74. Specialise in your photography by making a collection of your own photographs of birds, animals, seascapes, etc.

75. Photograph individual pieces of furniture you consider beautiful or interesting in your own home or elsewhere.

ART

76. Outdoor sketching. Farm buildings, old cottages, landscapes, seascapes, etc.

77. Plant drawing. Show by drawings the development of one or more plants week by week.

78. Make drawings from objects in museums. In London, the Natural History, Victoria and Albert, and British Museums. Many other towns possess very interesting museums.

79. Make wood blocks or linoleum blocks.

80. Illustrate any poem with paintings or drawings.

81. Visit any art or photography exhibitions in your district. Describe the pictures which most impress you.

82. Make a house sign, showing the name of your house, and if possible a pictorial representation of the name after the manner of the old shop and inn signs. Or make a full-sized drawing for one. Keep all drawing bold in outline, simple and brilliant in colouring.

83. Lettering. Make an alphabet in the best Roman, Italic, or Gothic style.

84. Visit the National Gallery and either describe or sketch certain features in old pictures—e.g. furniture, books, architecture, dress.

85. Design a wooden door handle or a wrought iron hinge, or a wooden entrance gate.

86. Design any article of furniture—e.g. table, chair, bedstead.

87. Go to one of the great London art galleries. Study the work of any great painter, and describe his pictures. Read his life and get reproductions of his pictures to illustrate your descriptions. The Watts pictures at the Tate Gallery would form a very fine collection to study.

88. Lettering. Make a book consisting of well-known prose passages, or poems.

89. Lettering. Write a poem or a prose extract on a piece of vellum, using red and black ink.

FOREIGN COUNTRIES

90. International Interests. Make a collection of illustrations from newspapers and other journals of current events in foreign countries.

91. Make a collection of illustrations dealing with any single foreign country.

92. If you go abroad, record all the new words or phrases you learn.

93. Write a short account of any foreign town you visit and illustrate with drawings and photographs, original or other. (Do not copy guide books: let your account be original.)

LANGUAGES

94. Make an illustrated French vocabulary by pasting pictures on one side of an exercise book and placing the meanings of various words you do not know which occur in the picture on the other side.

95. Learn ten French words a day. 500 during the holidays.

ARCHITECTURE

96. Design a window.
97. Design a gable.
98. Design a chimney.
99. Design the exterior of a cottage.

SOCIAL INVESTIGATIONS, ETC.

100. Write a description of the town you stay at during the holidays. Find out something of its history, churches, buildings, etc. Illustrate by photographs, drawings, or picture post-cards.

101. Write an account of local industries in any of the places you visit. There are frequently industries in connection with villages and small towns—e.g. basket-making at Beer, Dorset; pottery at Poole, and Compton in Surrey, etc.

102. In the case of bigger towns, write letters to managers, asking for permission to visit their works. Examples: gasworks, brickyards, cement mills, paper mills, iron foundries, blacksmiths, printers, saw mills. Write a descriptive and if possible illustrated account of what you see on these visits.

103. If you live in London or any other city, find out the open spaces available for the public within a radius of half a

mile from any given point. Draw a map of the district showing them. Try to estimate the population in the district.

104. If you live in a small town or village, find out any old inhabitants who can tell you legends, incidents, or stories connected with the district. Record these.

105. Describe the part played by your town or village in any epoch of history—e.g. the Civil War.

106. Write the history of any old building near your home. Illustrate with drawings or photographs.

107. Find out the number of unemployed in your town or district. Describe any relief works undertaken for their help. Make suggestions for other public work for their help.

108. Examine any of the working-class houses in your town which have been recently built. Criticise them.

109. Design a similar house yourself.

110. Visit the House of Commons both in and out of session and describe your impressions.

111. Visit the Law Courts and describe your impressions.

NATURAL HISTORY

112. Keep a daily diary recording all your observations of outdoor life.

113. Prepare an account of the chief birds found in England and illustrate your work by drawings or photographs.

114. Describe, from your original observations, the nests of different birds.

115. Describe any successes you have met with in encouraging birds to build near your own home.

116. Describe the notes of different birds.

117. Prepare an anthology of the best books on natural history in circulation to-day.

118. Make drawings of different forms of nesting-boxes for use in gardens.

119. Make drawings of different wild flowers.

120. Make drawings of moths and butterflies found in England; describe them.

121. Write an account from observations of the habits of some English bird (boys living near the coast could, for instance, study the various gulls).

122. Describe the life of a pond of sea water. Describe the life of a pond of fresh water.

123. Describe the best way of observing the habits of birds.

Chapter 16

AN EXPERIMENT IN
INTERNATIONAL EDUCATION

MORE than six months ago a group of boys in the school began to work at the construction of a model illustrating Dr Nansen's famous journey Farthest North. We began this piece of work as an act of homage to one of the great heroes of the world in which we live.

The making of the model followed the study by the members of the Scientific Society of the explorations undertaken by Dr Nansen. The work occupied many happy hours.

It was a considerable undertaking, being six feet square, and made to scale. It included subsidiary models of the *Fram*, the denizens of the Polar regions and other things.

It was completed last term, and a little party of boys with the head of the Science Department and myself went these holidays on a pilgrimage to Norway to present personally the model to Dr Nansen.

This is not the opportunity to tell in detail of the many interesting experiences we had. I must select those incidents which centre around the man we were visiting, and who had invited us to his house.

Dr Nansen's house stands on a hill a few miles from Oslo. It was at the end of winter when we saw it, and before the touch of spring had changed with its magic the desolate hills around. The trees as yet showed no sign of life. Only the famous Norwegian pines appeared green to relieve the wintry landscape. The house itself from the outside looked uninteresting. Its colour was drab and it lacked architectural charm. But inside the house was wholly delightful. Its windows looked beyond the near waters to the high hills in the background.

The house was designed by Dr Nansen, and its plan was admirable. There was a great living-room with a gallery above. From one side of this room you entered a set of rooms used by Dr Nansen for his work. From another side a dining-room and other rooms were entered through sliding doors. The dining-room was singularly beautiful. Its walls were covered by very striking frescoes illustrating a legend in the history of Norway. The artist had introduced Dr Nansen's own children into the paintings.

Our first interview with Dr Nansen was fixed to take place in the late afternoon of an early day after our arrival. The model was contained in a large case measuring more than six feet square. It had been an object of great anxiety to us all for we had transported it from Bembridge to far away Oslo, and at present it was lying in the courtyard of our hotel, that being the only place large enough to accommodate it. We mounted it on a motor lorry, most of the boys in the party scrambled to the top of it, and in this form we had something in the nature of a triumphal procession to the explorer's house, where we were anxious to unpack and prepare the model before its formal presentation. This we did, and all was ready in Dr Nansen's great hall at the hour appointed.

Perhaps I may be allowed to record the words in which the presentation to Dr Nansen was made:

We desire to ask your acceptance of this model, illustrating your great journey Farthest North, which has been made by members of Bembridge School.

Will you allow me, on behalf of the school, to attempt to record something of the gratitude we feel for the inspiration of your life and work. Some of us are too young to remember from contemporary accounts the days of your epic adventures in the arctic seas, but we have all read the imperishable story.

At the end of the war we remember that you led the civilised world in the attempt to fight the forces of disease, famine, and pestilence, which followed in its wake.

In those years, too, you took under your care the oppressed remnant of the Armenian nation, whose story is one of the tragedies of the world.

To-day you are the foremost champion of those who seek to make the brotherhood of nations a reality and to banish war from the earth.

We beg your acceptance of this gift, the work of our hands, as a symbol of our affection and homage.

Dr Nansen was greatly touched by the presentation, and made a very moving speech in reply. Every boy in our little party knew that a great friend was speaking to him. He spoke of their future, of what they might do in the world, of the need for peoples to come together, and of the good such visits as the present did.

After Dr Nansen had accepted the gift of the model, he examined it in great detail and told us many interesting things about his great journey.

Those who helped to make the model well remember how, in tracing upon it the route taken by the *Fram* when it was locked in the ice, at the mercy of unseen and unknown forces, to drift from one side of the world to the other, there came quite early in the journey a time when the *Fram* ceased to go forward and began to drift towards the position from which she had started. The explorer told us of the anxiety and disappointment which this brought to them all. If it continued it meant the negation of all their hopes, the destruction of all their plans. Could he have been mistaken? During those days of strain he went again through all his theories and the evidence which he thought proved their correctness. And as he did so he kept his faith that all would be well. There could be no failure now. What they had to do was to hold on. Soon he knew that he was right. The hostile winds were alone responsible for the strange backward movements of the ship. When these stopped the ship resumed her inexorable drift across the polar world.

Dr Nansen was particularly interested in that part of the model which showed Franz Joseph land which he reached with his solitary companion, after the weary months when he had left the *Fram* and had attempted to reach the North Pole on foot. He thought the land was very accurately shown on the model and was glad that the hills on this land were shown snow covered. For it was this snow which had prolonged his trials. He had probably seen this land for some weeks without recognising that it was land. He was conscious of a rather whiter atmosphere when he searched this part of the horizon, but it never struck him that it could be land. He was not at this time able to take accurate observations. His watch was wrong and there were other difficulties. Then one day he saw through his telescope two black spots where this line of a whiter colour appeared, and he realised he was looking at rocks emerging from the snow covered land.

On the day after this interview Dr Nansen sent me the following letter. It is addressed to the boys of Bembridge School, but I think it has a message far wider than this, for it is a message to all boys:

LYSAKER

19th April 1928

Dear Mr Whitehouse and my dear young friends,

It is difficult indeed to express the gratitude I feel, and to thank you as I should like to for this charming gift which you have built with your own hands and with your keen youthful interest, and then brought the long way to Norway and to Lysaker.

I am more touched than I can say by this admirable token of your sympathy and the interest you have taken in the work of our expedition in the *Fram*.

I must also express my admiration for the manner in which you have carried out your work and have stuck to it to the very end, and have finished it in every detail. And when it was finished you have yourselves taken the long journey to bring it to what you had decided to be its destination.

This is a remarkable proof of the right spirit in young people; an exquisite training for making men. It is only to be wished that there was much of it in the young generations. I do hope it will be the guiding spirit in the future life of all of you.

You are young, my friends, you have the life ahead of you with all its wonderful possibilities and adventure. I am sure that some day some of you may become great explorers in one field or other. We are all of us explorers in life whatever trail we follow.

But whether explorer or not, I have one advice to give you: stick to the work you begin in life, till the task is finished and finished well, whatever it may be. Go into it with your whole heart and your whole mind. Do not do things by halves, but carry your task through to the best of your ability, just as you have done this task; and be not satisfied before you have got the feeling that you cannot do it better. It is really remarkable how much you learn by doing a thing well. I am convinced that this is an important secret of real success in life, and it will give you the satisfactory feeling that you quit yourselves like men; for we have come here, in this world, every one of us, to do our part and to do it well.

It is men of that kind with the right stuff in them which the world now needs badly, and you, my young friends, will become some of them.

It is a difficult time you are living in, no doubt, and the world does not give you a bright outlook just now perhaps. But it is an interesting time, many important things are happening, and it is full of great problems for you to solve. It is you who have to create the future, and make the world a better place to live in.

A thing of special importance is, I think, to do all we can to create a better understanding and more confidence between nations, and in that way a fuller co-operation between them.

You have in your young age come to this country, I hope you will have a pleasant time here, and will return home with nice recollections of old Norway and her people, and with the feeling that you have visited a kindred race. And I do hope that that feeling will last for life, and that you will as men do your share to strengthen the good relations between your great people and ours, as well as all other peoples, and thus help to create a solid foundation for really wholesome international relations and for a betterment of the world.

I once more thank you from all my heart for your great gift and for your coming here and for all the kind sympathy and interest you have shown me.

Believe me, my dear friends,

Your grateful friend,

FRIDJOF NANSEN

We were all anxious to know from Dr Nansen what had happened to the *Fram*. He told us that it was in dock not far from Oslo, but he feared it was in danger of destruction. Owing to its special construction to withstand the ice pressure its timbers were closely wedged together in a way which did not allow proper ventilation. The result was that rot had set in. The only way to save it would be to put it in dry dock and have it extensively repaired and protected. It would be a very costly matter and the funds were not available.

He reminded us that after his own journey in the *Fram* she was used by Captain Sverdrop, his second in command on the *Fram*, for the arctic explorations he undertook. He had greatly altered it. The low deck, which was a feature of the ship originally, was quite suitable for the polar journey undertaken by Nansen, for he had not much open sea work to do. It was unsuitable for journeys in rough waters, for it meant that they were constantly shipping heavy seas with consequent discomfort and danger. The alteration was therefore a great improvement for Sverdrop's purposes.

After he had finished with the *Fram* it was used by Captain Amundsen, but few alterations were made by him in the design of the ship.

We learned from Dr Nansen with surprise and admiration that he hoped next year to go on an arctic expedition by airship. One was being built for him in Germany by sympathizers, who had undertaken that when completed it should be first placed at his disposal for the purpose of two journeys to the polar regions. The airship was being built so rapidly that he feared it would be ready long before he could start. In that case there might be a temptation to use it for other purposes first. He was anxious that when he was ready to start the airship should be in the finest condition. He wanted very much to go again on a polar expedition, and he thought an airship would be ideal for the purpose. It had a great lifting capacity—as much as a hundred tons, and therefore adequate stores could be carried.

An airship would also be fairly safe, for violent storms in the north polar regions were rare. The ship's anchors, fixed in the ice, would hold it securely when necessary.

Dr Nansen wanted particularly to take soundings in the polar seas. There was a great deal of scientific investigation waiting to be done.

It was my privilege to have much private conversation with Dr Nansen. Amongst the subjects we discussed was that of Armenia. He spoke at great length of his interest in the Armenians and his schemes for helping them. There were large numbers in Greece and Turkey living under unspeakable conditions. These should be moved to Armenia. He had had much trouble in connection with schemes for Armenian relief both with the English government and others. The League had entrusted the matter to him and had begged him to organise a scheme, but nearly all the members of the League had refused any financial help to carry out the scheme. He was so discouraged by this attitude that he had proposed at a recent meeting of the League that the scheme should be formally abandoned, for he did not think it consistent with the dignity of the League that they should have an official scheme which none of them supported. Nor was such a state of things of any help to the Armenians. But the League had persuaded him to continue his appeals for support for the scheme.

Since our conversation took place, I have received from Dr Nansen a copy of his book on Armenia, giving the record of his own journey to Armenia and to the Balkans and Turkey in connection with the relief of the Armenians. I have seldom read a more profoundly moving record. The massacres of the Armenians, beginning soon after the outbreak of the European war, and continuing long after it had finished, remain one of the greatest horrors that time has any record of.

I was able to discuss with Dr Nansen the American proposal for a multilateral pact for the renunciation of war. It was his earnest hope that the big nations of the world would sign the proposed treaty without hesitation. The mere signing of it would carry civilisation to a higher level. Nothing could be quite the same again.

Let me close this account of our visit by paying an inadequate tribute to the kindness and hospitality with which we were received by Dr Nansen. He established personal relations with each of our party, and every one soon knew him as a friend. When we embarked on our little steamer and sailed from Oslo, our last sight of him was as he waved us farewell from the quayside. That memory will always be in our minds, and there will be another beside it—the memory of Dr Nansen in his home above the fiords showing us his loved country, with his great happy dogs wildly gambolling around him.

We salute one of the great men of the world.

Chapter 17

IN FOREIGN FIELDS

IN recent years there has been an extraordinary increase in the number of English schoolboys going abroad, especially in the Christmas holidays, for purposes of sport. These sports holidays, within bounds, are good and healthy incidents in school life, but they must not be confused with the attempts which are being made, by means of foreign visits, to enable boys to understand something of the history, culture, and achievement of other peoples. A boy whose visits abroad are confined to sports centres meets for the most part people of his own country and is sometimes apt to have his sympathies warped rather than extended by incidents attendant upon crowded travel to fashionable places.

I believe profoundly in the value of foreign travel for boys, but I think if it is to have good results it must be something more than mere pleasure seeking. The pleasure will be the greater if there is some purpose behind the visit and if those in charge of it, without in any way making it into a school, or pressing unwelcome studies or knowledge upon those taking part, yet secure that there shall be a sympathetic interpretation of things worth seeing and knowing.

In our own school visits abroad have been a regular feature of its life. We have been to many places in France, we have been to Rome, Assisi, Venice, and other places in Italy, we have been to Holland, Norway and other countries. Our plan on all these journeys has been the same. We have spent the mornings in visiting galleries, museums, and other places and buildings of interest. In the afternoons our party has usually split up, all being given the opportunity of doing anything they wished.

We have found it much better in every way to settle at one place for at least a few days rather than to attempt a continuous pilgrimage.

One advantage of this method is that we get away from the motor car habit, of which so many boys are now victims. We substitute for blurred, dusty, tired impressions, memories of restful stays in little towns, of kind country people, of beautiful pictures and haunting gardens, above all of human friendship.

Here is a typical diary of one of our foreign visits. This was one to Holland in 1927.

"*Friday*, April 29th. We had arranged to travel by a large liner, the Orania, coming from South America, and after calling at Southampton, going direct to Amsterdam. The only drawback to this arrangement was some uncertainty as to the time it would touch at Southampton. We were first advised that we should assemble at 2 o'clock. Later the agents telephoned that we must be ready to embark at 12 o'clock, and we were all at the dock gates by this hour. But the liner dallied and we were able to lunch in Southampton before it arrived, for we did not embark until 4.30, going in a tender almost to Cowes before meeting our ship.

We had comfortable airy cabins, the sea was perfectly calm, and we all had a good night (including one who describes himself without exaggeration as the worst sailor in Europe).

Saturday, April 30th. We awoke to find our fine weather continuing and we passed a happy day at sea, making ourselves acquainted with every part of the ship. The most exciting part of the voyage was three or four hours before reaching Amsterdam, when we passed through the great lock admitting us to the wonderful North Sea canal, completed in 1876, which secured the permanence of Amsterdam as a port. The canal, fifteen miles long, is one of the most striking engineering achievements of modern times.

We reached Amsterdam in the early morning and walked to our hotel in the Auchterburgwal, a street with a canal running down the middle of it, and lined with picturesque houses of the traditional Dutch style. We were glad of dinner, and later made some tentative explorations of our magical surroundings.

Sunday, May 1st. David Croll arrived early in the day from Rotterdam, smiling and debonair. We gave him the warmest of welcomes. Under his guidance we spent the morning exploring the city, and in the East end we saw the famous Jews' market. The customs were quaint. Many people bought long pickled fishes from street costermongers, and holding them at one end began to nibble at them until they had disappeared! We turned with relief to the pedlars in eggs who cooked and distributed these in the middle of large crowds.

We visited the house where Rembrandt lived. A large crowd assembled to watch us ascend the steps of the house and for a moment it seemed that a great popular demonstration in our honour was to take place. Fortunately this was averted.

In the afternoon we visited the Rijks Museum, containing the most famous collection of pictures in Amsterdam. The works of two great artists specially impressed us, the glorious Rembrandts and the pictures of Dutch interiors by Pieter de Hooch. Perhaps the two greatest features of Rembrandt's work are his power as a portrait painter and his wonderful colours. The interiors by Hooch have at once delicacy and realism and are indescribably beautiful.

From the windows of the museum we had a good view of the impressive May Day Labour procession. It included many thousands of men, women and children, numerous bands and a wealth of banners with mottoes and exhortations. 'Read your own press,' 'Disarm,' 'We want the 8 hours' day,' are some translations of the latter. The procession must have been some miles in length, for although we watched it for a long time, when we left it was still unexhausted. Its mere size made it imposing.

Monday, May 2nd. In the morning we went to the famous Zoological Gardens on the outskirts of Amsterdam. The grounds were well laid out and arranged. One experience alone made us rejoice that we had included the Zoo in our pilgrimage. We assembled before a large friendly elephant who came forward and held out his trunk for offerings. We gave him grass and other tit-bits which he conveyed to his mouth. Then there was a brief interval. Suddenly the elephant scooped up in his trunk a large quantity of gravel and sand and hurled it at us, catching and covering some of us. We fled, and then approached him very gingerly. He tried to show us that he was only having a game, and in order to encourage us he scooped up more gravel and sand and flung it over himself. As soon however as we had recovered confidence and got near enough, he again attacked us with the gravel and on one occasion completely smothered Mr Baggaley. Every effort was made to induce the elephant to repeat this special part of the performance.

In the afternoon we visited the Municipal Museum. This will always be memorable to us on account of the pictures by Israels. To most of us he was a name only, and perhaps not that, but his paintings contained in the museum enabled us to realise that Israels was one of the great modern masters. Surely at few times in the history of art have simple, human scenes and emotions been painted with more sympathy and understanding. To see his pictures is not only to be at once conquered by their appeal, but one instinctively realises also that only a man of great qualities could have painted them.

On *Tuesday*, May 3rd, we went first to the University Library in Amsterdam. We were received with very great courtesy by the director of the library and shown through all its departments. This library is intended primarily for serious students and contains one million books. The chief divisions of the library are contained in separate rooms which is a great help to the student. The director kindly arranged in one of the rooms the chief manuscripts possessed by the library, and these were a source of great interest to all of us. We were also astonished at the freedom from dust in the library. The musty, dusty atmosphere which is frequently associated with old books was wholly absent.

In the afternoon we went by train to Haarlem. The town hall at Haarlem is an extremely interesting building, and the chief room inside was beautiful with old oak beams, old furniture and some fine tapestry. We went also to the 15th century church. I do not think this approached similar buildings in France, or England, but it had an interest of its own. The interior was marred by an organ which, though it may have been very beautiful when played, was an example of atrocious colouring and architecture.

Wednesday, May 4th. This morning we took a tram car from the centre of Amsterdam to the suburbs of the city. Leaving the car we walked towards the great dam which protects Amsterdam from the encroaching sea. We had to content ourselves with a view of the dam in the distance, for it was too far off for us to reach it within the time at our disposal.

After an early lunch at the hotel we said good-bye to Amsterdam and took a train to the Hague. What would otherwise have been a very ordinary journey became a wonderful experience because we travelled through some miles of bulb gardens, and to see these great flaming masses in beds that extended for miles was an experience never to be forgotten. It is, I suppose, a sight that no other European country could offer. Miniature railways ran to some of these gardens and the trucks were being laden with the flowers, but we had eyes for nothing except this glorious feast of colour.

At the Hague we found our headquarters at a very comfortable hotel, the Hôtel du Passage. We were to go on to Rotterdam on the following day, so we saw as much of the Hague as possible in the afternoon and evening. One feature is worth recording which we observed not only at the Hague, but everywhere we went in Holland: the almost universal habit of travelling by bicycle. There are no hills to negotiate and motor cars are not yet sufficiently numerous to make cycling in a city equivalent to suicide as in this country. We spent a long evening exploring the city, and particularly the old buildings around the Royal Palace.

Thursday, May 5th. After breakfast this morning we went to the famous picture gallery in the Mauritshuis. Our attention was chiefly claimed in this wonderful art gallery by the works of two masters, Rembrandt and Vermeer. We were able to study perhaps the most famous of all Rembrandt's paintings, his School of Anatomy, and although the subject is not one which at first sight would appear to be suitable for permanent representation on canvas, it is singularly free from repulsiveness and is really a most magnificent example of portraiture. Of the works by Rembrandt one of the most impressive is Homer, showing the blind poet dictating verses to the sound of the lyre.

Jan Vermeer has only recently become very famous in Holland. Now there are few artists held in greater regard. His chief work is contained in this museum, a famous view of Delft. Vermeer lived in Holland chiefly at Delft, from 1632–1675. In the 19th and 20th centuries few pictures have exercised a more powerful influence on landscape painting. It is idle to attempt to describe it. It is pure joy to look at a picture so restful and satisfying, yet so real with wonderful effects of light and shade and great brilliance of colouring.

We tore ourselves from the gallery with reluctance and went by train to Rotterdam, arriving there at midday. We were met by David Croll and his father. They took us to their beautiful home in the suburbs of the city where we had lunch in a delightful garden of typical Dutch beauty and restfulness. After lunch Mr Croll took us in a motor launch through Rotterdam harbour, which was in itself a wonderful experience.

We were greatly impressed by the size and extent of the docks and the enormous trade which was being done with all parts of the world. We saw vessels under construction, and we saw a newly completed bridge which is one of the chief engineering feats of modern times, for the whole of this great bridge except its supporting sides can be raised bodily in order to allow ships to pass underneath. It is as though the Tower Bridge over the Thames, instead of opening in the centre, was pulled up on high columns. We returned from our cruise and were entertained to tea by Mr Croll at a club house overlooking the harbour. We must record our indebtedness to Mr and Mrs Croll and to David for their unlimited hospitality which made our last day in Holland also the most notable.

After tea we went by train to the Hook of Holland and boarded our steamer for Harwich."

Chapter 18

SOME REFLECTIONS AND SUGGESTIONS

IN the brief survey which I have tried to give in the preceding pages of some features of what I have called creative education, I have contented myself with speaking of actual experiments carried out and work done.

I should like in this final chapter to offer for consideration and discussion some suggestions affecting the whole field of English education.

I want to appeal first for a wider curriculum. In the valuable report of the Consultative Committee on the Education of Adolescents, which marks in the main a great advance in educational theory, I am concerned that one proposal which the committee makes, the foundation of what are to be called grammar schools on the one side, and modern schools on the other, should be carefully examined. It would, I think, be a great obstacle to educational advance if anything were done to standardise or to make more rigid the scheme of education either in the old grammar schools, the old secondary schools or the new modern schools. So far from making the curriculum of these schools more rigid, we want to make it much more elastic, much more experimental.

We want to do this by means of a wider curriculum and by the introduction of a far greater number of manual activities. We should be wrong if we assumed that the main means of education is through book learning, or by going along narrow academic lines. Perhaps we have never adequately realised that manual activities properly conceived are most valuable instruments of education. We ought no longer to consider these as suitable only for little children. We ought to make appropriate use of such activities at every stage of education.

I venture to appeal for a re-consideration of the function of examinations. I think examinations are necessary both within the school, and from without. We ought not however to regard the method and scope of examinations as at present constituted as the final machinery of the educational world.

I was greatly impressed recently in discussing this question with the headmaster of an important grammar school. We had been considering creative activities, and he had been looking at some of those which I have described. He had then put before me his position as the headmaster of a great grammar school, an endowed grammar school, where, he told me, he was entirely controlled by the examination system at present in vogue. I need not refer to any particular examination; it is the principle to which I am referring. He told me this, that practically the whole of the boys in his school took a certain examination at a certain age; that he could not vary his curriculum; he could not introduce these other activities, however profoundly he believed in them—it was a day school—because it would encroach upon the time necessary for cramming for this examination and would meet with general hostility. He also told me, what I hope is not generally true, but what he assured me was true in his own school, that the boys themselves resented having their attention diverted from the actual examination subjects, being keen to pass the examination and obtain the necessary certificate, but that they followed the subjects without any real zest or interest, and certainly got no pleasure or joy from them.

This experience of one whose judgment would carry great weight with all who knew him, if at all general, gives special point to one suggestion respecting examinations which I think should not be difficult quickly to carry out. They should immediately be so broadened that it would be possible to present for examination the work of pupils in such a way as to enable the original creative work which they have done in art, craftsmanship, and other spheres, to be judged, and to receive at least the same honour as is given to other forms of work.

In this way, and only in this way, will it be possible to prevent a stereotyped system of examinations from controlling the curriculum of schools. In this way it will be possible to do more justice to those who teach. They have not been allowed sufficient liberty, and above all, they have not been allowed to give full play to the potential capacities of their pupils. In this way honour will be given to art, craftsmanship, and the creative activities generally.

I desire to record my conviction that the teaching of drawing is essential to all forms of education. It is an instrument which is as important to the pupil as writing, and more important than many things we consider essential. It is at once a method of education, the acquisition of a new medium of communication, the gaining of the power of observation, and it develops some of the highest gifts of personality. It should not be regarded as a little boy's hobby. It should not be given with an air of tolerance an inferior place in examination schemes. In some of these latter it is not allowed any value and is placed in a position inferior to that given to very elementary forms of arithmetic, or simple geographical knowledge.

It should be treated with an honour not less than that given to any subject. It should accompany education at all its stages.

Manual activities have a singularly broadening influence. They can be so used as to create the spirit of sympathy and tolerance, and above all to give real values in life even during schooldays. They give boys hobbies which become real interests. They enable boys who have few academic gifts to retain their self-respect because they find other ways of self-expression. They give boys intellectually brilliant greater culture and a truer and wider vision.

I believe all who have the care of young people will be inclined to agree with me when I state that games are not a sufficient method of meeting the needs of boys in their leisure hours. The good of games is obvious, and I have had the opportunity more than once of speaking of their discipline, the joy which they create, the exercise in chivalry and unselfishness: the health and bodily fitness for which they stand. But when all this has been said, a profound mistake has been made if the leisure hours of schoolboys are filled only with games. That is the way to give false values.

It is through the activities of school life that such interests should be aroused as will enable boys to express their gifts and individuality in those hours when their lives are not organised or controlled. Games will then take their proper place in the life of a boy, and in the life of the community.

Every new interest which we introduce into the life of children, every serious interest, may be the means of giving them a more spacious spiritual life. Every new interest we give them relieves them from the temptation to idleness and baser pleasures, and enables them to pursue life with standards of taste and criticism, with real interests of their own. The great division between the educated and the uneducated is really the division between those who have noble interests in life and those who have none. These creative activities unlock for them new doors to avenues of interest and real work.

I am not writing a general treatise on education. I am trying to give a record of some few things which have been attempted and done. But I should like to add this. It is not unreasonable to submit that a school should aim at certain definite objects, and amongst these objects I suggest that the following should have a place of honour. A boy who has passed through a public school should have been encouraged to attain perfect physical health. His outlook should be wider than that shown by one who cares only for the commercial value of success in a little panel of subjects. He should love knowledge and be interested sufficiently to work hard to secure it. He should have standards of true values in a world which listens contentedly either to the broadcasting of the raucous voices of the race course or the singing of the nightingale. He should be able to use at least the simpler forms of drawing if only because it is an additional instrument of communication, of keeping in touch with the wonders of the world; at the least a means of observation.

He should be trained in the use of tools, and should be able to share with the great men of all time the joy of creative activity. He should have the opportunity of pursuing his own individual interests. He should not only love but be able to understand the grounds for his love of noble literature, art, music, nature, the beauty of the simple, yet final things in human life, love, toleration, charity. He should know from travel and from history something of the world in which he is to live and work, and his knowledge should lead him to the love of peace and the realisation of the kinship of men in all countries.

He should realise the need of service, the call to share his gifts with others. Above all he should realise the sanctity of work, and he should be able to fill the broad spaces of his time with activities at once noble and well directed.

This does not mean an easy life. It does not mean soft options at school, the avoidance of difficult subjects. It means sincerity and courage in facing difficulty. It is a call to the strenuous life in all its aspects.

And that is the way of happiness.

EPILOGUE

One word remains to be said. A school is composed of a thousand influences. There is no short cut to success. It is always striving after the ideal, with youthful pilgrims who are ever changing. As I conclude this book I wish to express my gratitude to the staff of the school who help to sustain these young adventurers in many byeways.

And especially I wish to thank Edward Daws, the sub-warden, who has brought the production of school plays to a remarkable degree of beauty; Ernest J. Baggaley, who has inspired a love for science which extends far beyond the laboratories; Ronald C. Muirhead, who has enabled boys to fill their leisure hours with real interests; Reginald Hughes, who gives to art the devotion of his life; Miss Kingsnorth, who has fired young boys with a real appreciation of beautiful things; T. Raymond Parsons, who has revived the glories of one of the oldest arts; Wilfrid Grace, who has given young boys a love for English literature.

Our mother service — I, the son,
As you the daughter of our land!'
Three mornings more, she took her stand
In the same place, with the same eyes:
I was no surer of sun-rise
Than of her coming: we conferred
Of her own prospects, and I heard
She had a lover — stout and tall,
She said — then let her eyelids fall,
'He could do much' — as if some doubt
Entered her heart, — then, passing out,
'She could not speak for others, who
Had other thoughts: herself she knew:'
And so she brought me drink and food.
After four days, the scouts pursued
Another path; at last arrived
The help my Paduan friends contrived.

Example of Writing and Illumination   by John Freeman

Nature Study Drawing

Imaginative Sketch of Church Interior

The Pied Piper of Hamelin.   by. R. Browning.

Hamelin Town's in Brunswick,
     By famous Hanover city;
The river Weser, deep and wide,
Washes its wall on the southern side;
A pleasanter spot you never spied;
     But, when begins my ditty,
Almost five hundred years ago,
To see the townsfolk suffer so
     From vermin, was a pitty.

Rats!
They fought the dogs and killed the cats,
     And bit the babies in the cradles
And ate the cheeses out of the vats,
     And licked the soup from the cook's own ladles,
Split open the kegs of salted sprats,
Made nests inside men's Sunday hats,
And even spoiled the women's chats
     By drowning their speaking
     With shrieking and squeaking
In fifty different sharps and flats.

A page from a commonplace book   by John Flugel

Few leisure time pursuits have given the author of this book greater
encouragement than that which he has got from the literary enthusiasm
shown by many boys who have kept commonplace books of remarkable
variety and interest.

THE ITALIAN
IN ENGLAND

ROBERT BROWNING

A Book Cover designed and lettered   by John Freeman

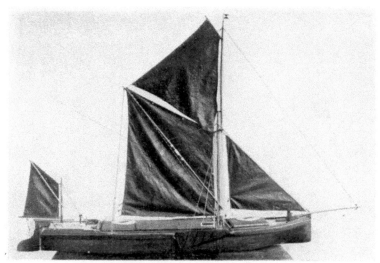

Model of Thames Barge   by John Brandon-Jones

This, and the other models, which are reproduced in this book, illustrate work done by boys in their leisure hours. Such work may not be formally taught, but the interest in it naturally arises through providing the opportunity for self-expression.

BRITISH WILD FLOWERS.

Design for Cover

Culver Cliff from the Forelands

Water colour drawing   by Adrian Beach

Model of Canal Boat   by John Brandon-Jones

Sculpture in stone   by Darsie Rawlins

This is an example of what may be done by a boy who is given the
opportunity to express his own individuality and follow up his special
interests.

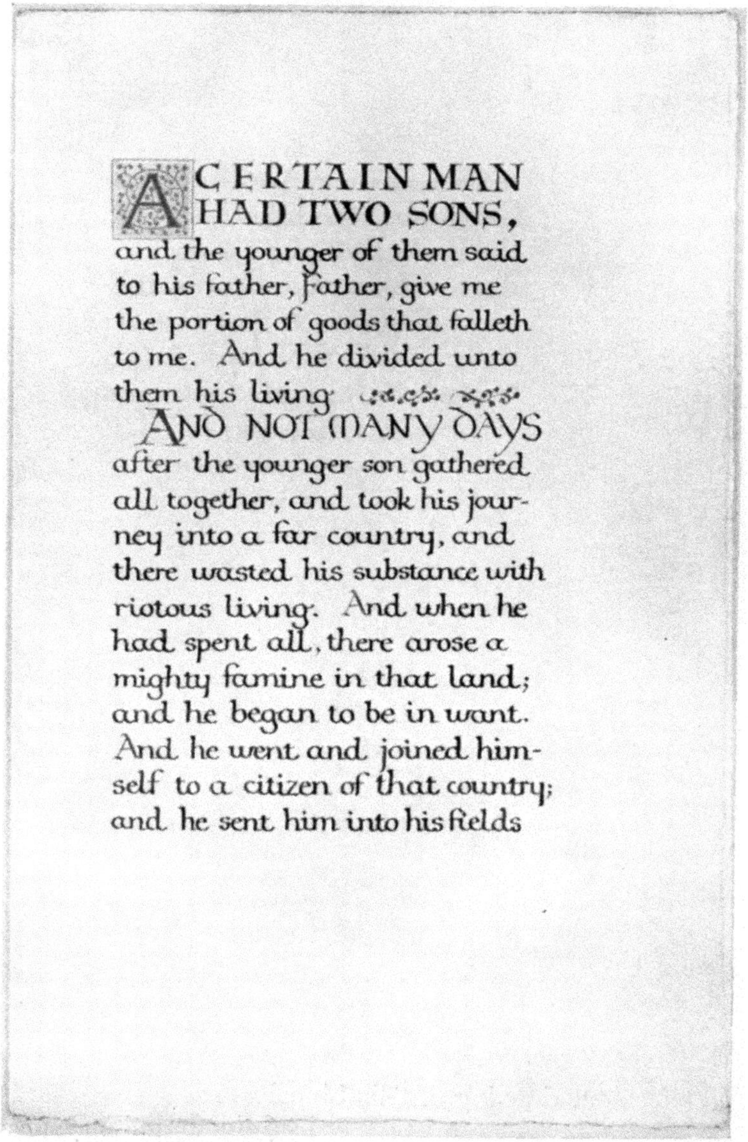

A CERTAIN MAN
HAD TWO SONS,
and the younger of them said
to his father, Father, give me
the portion of goods that falleth
to me. And he divided unto
them his living ❧ ❧
AND NOT MANY DAYS
after the younger son gathered
all together, and took his journey into a far country, and
there wasted his substance with
riotous living. And when he
had spent all, there arose a
mighty famine in that land;
and he began to be in want.
And he went and joined himself to a citizen of that country;
and he sent him into his fields

Example of Writing & Illumination   by John Freeman

Water colour drawing of Climbing Rose
by John Brandon-Jones

It illustrates the attempt made whenever possible to unite drawing with
the observation of nature.

And he is bright and pleasant and very mighty and strong. ∿∿ Praised be my Lord for our mother the earth, the which doth sustain us and keep us, and bringeth forth divers fruits and grasses and flowers of many colors. Praised be my Lord for all those who pardon one another for his love's sake, and who endure weakness and tribulation; blessed are they who

Illuminated Page   by Michael Relph (aged 12)

This is a simple example showing how literature, art, nature study and writing, may all be united in the drawing periods of form room work.

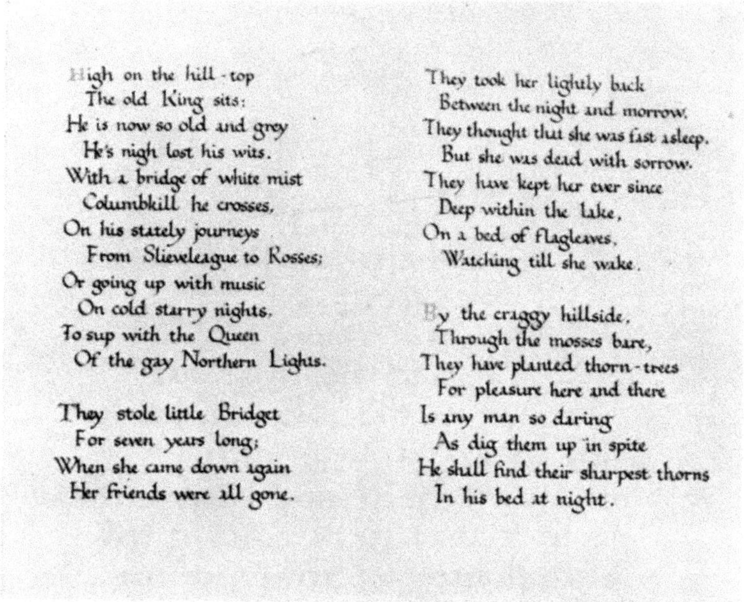

High on the hill-top
  The old King sits;
He is now so old and grey
  He's nigh lost his wits.
With a bridge of white mist
  Columbkill he crosses,
On his stately journeys
  From Slieveleague to Rosses;
Or going up with music
  On cold starry nights,
To sup with the Queen
  Of the gay Northern Lights.

They stole little Bridget
  For seven years long;
When she came down again
  Her friends were all gone.

They took her lightly back
  Between the night and morrow,
They thought that she was fast asleep,
  But she was dead with sorrow.
They have kept her ever since
  Deep within the lake,
On a bed of flagleaves,
  Watching till she wake.

By the craggy hillside,
  Through the mosses bare,
They have planted thorn-trees
  For pleasure here and there
Is any man so daring
  As dig them up in spite
He shall find their sharpest thorns
  In his bed at night.

Example of Writing   by John Freeman
The capitals were done in gold

Culver Cliff

Water colour   by Adrian Beach

Cloud and sea effects

Water colour drawing   by Adrian Beach

Boat built by John Brandon-Jones & Roger Wilkinson

Weathercock   by John Brandon-Jones

Sea and Rocks

Water colour drawing   by Adrian Beach

Sculpture in stone   by Darsie Rawlins

Buckler's Hard

Pencil drawing   by R. C. Shotter

Coast Scene   by Adrian Beach
Water colour drawing

Model of Barn executed in oak by John Brandon-Jones

This model was designed by the boy who built it; the roof is covered with some thousands of oak shingles, each one cut by hand. It forms the setting for a nativity group

Design for a Calendar

Animals carved in wood   by Adrian Beach

Large Scale Model of Mount Everest

Made by a group of boys to illustrate the story of the Expedition to try
to reach the Summit

Initial Letters in water colour　　　by C. L. Barbezat

A Batsman's Nightmare

Pencil and ink drawing   by John Flugel

Boy with pony

Many of the boys have the opportunity of riding. This makes
an important addition to joyous healthy exercise

Boy in study: the furniture and
fittings, except chair, were made
by the boys

Photograph of Tit   by H. P. Rose

Example of nature study photography

Boy at lathe

This pole lathe was made by
the boys, and much good work
has been done on it

Canoe building: painting

The two brothers in the photograph built the canoe

Water colour drawing   New School House   by Adrian Beach

114

From a photograph

Junior School Gardens

Rest period

After the midday meal, the custom of having a rest period
for half an hour gives boys the opportunity for reading,
nature study and other quiet occupations

The School Pottery: examples of work done by the boys

The School Pottery: the kiln
packed for firing. From a boy's
photograph

Examples of Pottery

Through the practice of pottery boys gain further standards for the appreciation of beauty in form and colour

Canoe and its builder

Gymnasium, garden and pool, water colour   by Adrian Beach

This garden was the work of one boy

At Oslo, April 1928

These boys were conveying to Dr Nansen a model
made at the school illustrating his journey Farthest
North

A corner of the Junior House Gardens
Water colour drawing   by Adrian Beach

Boat building

The boat was designed and built by the boys shown

Boat building: finishing touches

Sailing in the school bay

The boat shown in the two preceding photographs with its
builders

Illustration to "Our Lady's Juggler"

Water colour   by Michael Relph

A Dormitory

Water colour   by S. Hill

Drawing of Living Room, New School House
Water colour   by Anthony Holloway

A corner of Big Dormitory, New School House
Water colour   by Anthony Holloway

An Early Morning Ride   School photograph

"When the boy is seven years old he has to go and learn all about horses, and is taught by the masters of horsemanship, and begins to go against wild beasts; and when he is fourteen years old, they give him the masters whom they call the Kingly Child-Guiders: and these are four, chosen the best out of all the Persians who are then in the prime of life—to wit, the most wise man they can find, and the most just, and the most temperate, and the most brave; of whom the first, the wisest, teaches the prince the magic of Zoroaster; and that magic is the service of the Gods: also he teaches him the duties that belong to a king. Then the second, the justest, teaches him to speak truth all his life through. Then the third, the most temperate, teaches him not to be conquered by even so much as a single one of the pleasures, that he may be exercised in freedom, and verily a king, master of all things within himself, not slave to them. And the fourth, the bravest, teaches him to be dreadless of all things, as knowing that whenever he fears, he is a slave."

PLATO

Flower Studies
May 22, 1925
by John Major
Form III.

Flower Studies   Water colour by John Major

A very rare scene is on a very hot sultry day in early summer, when you are lying with your head over a chalk cliff. On the horizon is some smoke slowly rising from some passing ship. Far down below, the green sea laps against the rocks and falls back as if it is tired. All around gulls are swooping, flying and

A page from a School Diary, kept by the boys, recording the activities of the term

A page from a book illustrating The Ancient Mariner

Water colour   by Norman Flowers

This is a further example of group work in the production of an illustrated book

Chart illustrating Shakespeare's Life and Times by John Flugel

Reference is made earlier in this book to the place of charts as a help to the historical imagination

from imagination.

Cinderella   by Darsie Rawlins

Illustration to a book of fairy tales made and decorated by a group of boys working in co-operation

Corner of Boy's Room

The cupboards, writing desk, wainscoting and decoration, were done by the boys occupying the room

Small table by H. Wright made and designed in the
arts and crafts room

As in other cases the turning was done on a pole lathe

Gate-leg table in Oak made by C. R. Bishop

The turning of the legs was done on a pole lathe made by the boys

Bedstead in Oak designed and made in the school
arts and crafts room by J. R. Barker

A boy's contribution to the annual exhibition of school work

Bookshelves in Oak, made by R. A. Jones
in the arts and crafts room

In all the woodwork done throughout the school an attempt is made to enable
boys to understand the principles of beauty and their dependence upon good
craftsmanship

School bed and cabinet, made by boys in the wood-work room

Reduced facsimile of the School
Newspaper printed by the boys on
the school press each Term.

The size of the newspaper is $10 \times 7\frac{1}{2}$ inches
and contains about 40 pages

The design on the cover changes each Term.
Both the lettering and the pictures are from
woodcuts done by the boys

The Harbour
by Anthony Holloway

Invocation   by John Barker

The Stairway   by Adrian Beach

The Trawler   by John Brandon-Jones

A Rough Sea   by Anthony Holloway

The Bridge
by John Brandon-Jones

The Abbey   by Adrian Beach

Solitude   by Sam Hill

Floods   by Adrian Beach

The Fisherman's Hut   by Adrian Beach

The Miner   by Sam Hill

The Mother
   by Adrian Beach

Lobster Fishers   by Anthony Holloway

A Peaceful Scene   by Anthony Holloway

The Arrow
by Darsie Rawlins

St George   by Adrian Beach

What you will   by Adrian Beach

The Stoker
by Darsie Rawlins

St Francis

Initial Letter

Old Fashions

Blocks designed by Adrian Beach
and cut by Vincent Beach

The Redskin   by Sam Hill

The Mill

by Adrian Beach

The Pied Piper   by Sam Hill

The Sailing Ship   by Anthony Holloway

For EU product safety concerns, contact us at Calle de José Abascal, 56–1°, 28003 Madrid, Spain or eugpsr@cambridge.org.